DISCOVERING
QATAR

FRANCES GILLESPIE

Sponsored by

RasGas Company Limited

First published: 2006

Editing and Design by Marijcke Jongbloed
Photo scanning and Printing by Colorlines, Dubai
Published by Creative Writing and Photography, 1 LD Fougirard, 33580 Rimons, France

ISBN 99921-70-32-8

Captions pictures: front cover: main picture: Cistanche tubulosa
inset left: Al Wajba fort, inset right: Rueppell's fox
back cover: left: al Murrah girl spinning wool
right top: turtle hatchling, right bottom: jalbut
title page: Calendula arvensis

Contents

Background: Cistanche tubulosa

Dedication

To Marijcke Jongbloed M.D., resident in the UAE 1983 — 2003,
in gratitude for all the advice, help and encouragement over the years.

*F*OREWORD

TRADITIONALLY OCCUPIED BY BEDOUINS, THE STATE OF QATAR HAS A LONG HISTORY of developing its economy utilising its natural resources. The discovery of oil and natural gas has contributed to the rapid transformation of the State of Qatar, positioning it as a vibrant economy on the world stage.

Whilst Qatar is committed to a programme of sustainable development through all sectors of the community it has not forgotten its history. The nomadic life of the desert-dwelling Bedouin, pearling, fishing and trade by land and sea sustained the people of Qatar for centuries. The success of Qatar is firmly rooted in strong traditions and a rich culture all of which are remembered and acknowledged. This book, Discovering Qatar by Frances Gillespie celebrates the traditional lifestyle and history of Qatar.

Qatar is a land of many secrets and ecological delights. From the air, first impressions of the peninsula are of a flat, barren, sandy desert surrounded by shallow seas. But the territory, both marine and terrestrial, is of great scientific beauty and interest. Aspects of its abundant and fascinating topography, geology, fauna and vegetation all find a deserved place within these pages.

In this rapidly developing region, the future of the fragile environment is dependent upon our understanding and observation of conservation needs. RasGas sees its responsibility for the preservation of the environment as a core commitment, and is pleased to be associated with this book, which it is hoped will inspire more people to share the fascinating history, culture and natural heritage of Qatar.

Dr. Mohammed Saleh al Sada
Managing Director
Rasgas Company Limited

Arabian Leopard Trust (C&M Stuart, R. Llewellyn-Smith, U. Wernery): 81 inset, 82, 83, 85, 86 top, 94

Agius, Dionisius: bc right bottom, 22, 41, 43, 44, 45, 46 bottom, 47, 48 bottom, 50, 51

Baldwin, Robert: fc main picture, 127, 128, 129, 130, 133 top, 134 bottom, 135, 136, 138, 140, 141, 142

Brown, bBsh: 90 bottom, 97, 104 bottom, 133 bottom, 134 top

Centre for Geographic Information Systems, Doha, Qatar: x, 53 bottom, 69, 70, 71 top, 74 right, 75 right, 76

Gardner, Drew: 91 inset, 94, 95, 96 top, 98 top, 102, 103 top, 104 top, 106, 107, 109

Gillespie, David: fc left inset, iv, v, viii, x, 1, 2, 4, 7, 11, 12, 15, 16, 18, 20, 21, 23, 24, 32, 33, 37 bottom, 46 right, 52, 53, 55, 56, 57, 58, 65, 66, 68, 73, 74 left, 75 left, 80, 87 inset, 102 top, 111, 113 bottom, 114

Gillespie, Frances: 27 bottom middle and right, 28 bottom, 29

Johnson Dennis: 119

Jongbloed, Marijcke: fc right inset, i, iii, vi, vii, 59 bottom, 64 background, 67, 71 bottom, 72, 77, 78, 79, 81, 82 inset, 87, 88, 89, 90, 91, 92, 93, 96 bottom, 98 bottom, 99, 100, 101, 103 inset, 103 bottom, 105, 106 inset, 108, 110, 112, 113t op, 114, 116, 121, 126, 139, 144, 148

Kay, Shirley: 34, 35, 48 top, 49

Larkworthy, Maria: 14

Moesgard Museum, Denmark (Klaus Ferdinand and Jette Bang): back cover left, 58 inset, 59, 60, 61, 62 top, 63, 64 inset

National Council for Culture, Arts and Heritage, Doha, Qatar: 3, 5, 6, 8, 9, 10, 17, 19, 25 bottom, 26, 27 bottom left, 28 top, 31 36, 37, 38, 39, 40, 41, 42

Pilcher, Nick: bc right top, 122, 123, 124, 125

Schwartz, Henning: 115, 116, 117, 118, 120

Van der Weg, Minie: 13

Above: Launaea capitata

INTRODUCTION

IN THIS BOOK I HAVE ATTEMPTED TO OUTLINE THE PREHISTORY AND HISTORY OF QATAR, give a brief introduction to its topography, and of aspects of its natural fauna which have interested me over the years. My aim is to enable others to share some of these interests, and to enjoy to the full their stay in hospitable, friendly Qatar, however long or short it may be.

When I arrived in Qatar with my family in August 1985, I knew almost nothing about the desert landscape of Arabia and its inhabitants, human or otherwise. As soon as the temperature dropped enough to allow exploration, we set out on what has proved to be a twenty-year expedition, and one that has still to be completed. Small though the peninsula of Qatar is, there are still far-off corners that remain to be fully explored.

We had come from the steaming, tropical rainforest region of West Africa, and I quickly grew to love the wide open spaces of Qatar, the way the immense sky met the far horizon, the ever-changing colours of the shadows on the great dunes of the south, the strange golden landscape studded with shining white limestone *mesas* along the western coast. We liked, too, exploring the little coastal villages with their friendly people, and watching the fleets of fishing dhows which set off at sun-set from Al Wakra, Al Khor and Al Ruwais. Doha in those days was a quiet city with comparatively little traffic, a shadow of the bustling 21st century metropolis it has now become.

Everywhere on the floor of the sandy desert I could see patterns left by myriads of small feet, like writing in a foreign language waiting to be interpreted. I knew so little about Arabian animals that the first time I saw a hedgehog I took it for a juvenile, not realising that Arabian mammals are smaller than their European cousins. Small, thin fragments of what looked a little like Chinese porcelain, but clearly was not, which we found on old settlement sites, puzzled me mightily until one day I learned that within the last century a species of ostrich unique to Arabia had roamed the plains of Qatar.

Arthrocnemum macrostachyum, a saltbush

There was a lot of learning to do, and finding sources of information about all the wildlife was at first not easy. We joined the Qatar Natural History Group and there followed many years of Friday expeditions, guided by amateur ornithologists and botanists and sometimes by geologists from the oil companies, who were ever ready to share their knowledge with others.

A study of the ecology and flora of Qatar had been published by the University of Qatar in 1981, and soon after we arrived the Ministry of Information issued a useful guide, *Qatar and the Sea*, written by a marine biologist at the National Museum, which included colour photographs of fish, cetaceans and sea snakes. But it seemed that little was available on the terrestrial mammals and reptiles of Arabia for the general reader.

Then in 1987, Marijcke Jongbloed, a Dutch doctor based in the UAE, published *The Living Desert*, a fascinating month-by-month guide to the plants, insects, reptiles, birds and mammals she had encountered on her peregrinations. These had first appeared as weekly articles in the Khaleej Times. For years, this book accompanied us everywhere on our weekend excursions.
Dr Jongbloed produced more books on the natural history of the Emirates in the next few years, and much

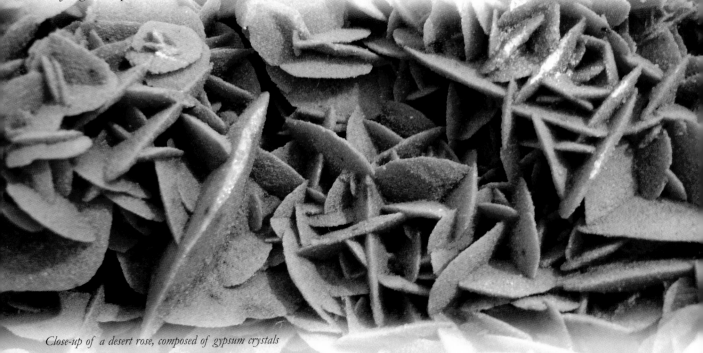

Close-up of a desert rose, composed of gypsum crystals

of what she wrote about applied to Qatar. She was appointed Director of the state-of-the-art Sharjah Natural History Museum and I invited her to lecture to our Natural History Group. We became friends, and over the years I relied on her for information. Most encouraging of all was the fact that she, beginning as a complete amateur, became in time renowned as an authority on the natural history of the region.

For ten years I have contributed features on all aspects of natural history and the environment, as well as on the archaeology and history of Qatar, to the Gulf Times newspaper, and, following the example set by Dr Jongbloed, this book has grown out of these articles. My study of the country's archaeology was assisted by the staff of the National Museum, who allowed me access to all excavation reports, both published and unpublished. Over the years I met most of the archaeologists who had worked in Qatar, including the pioneers Geoffrey Bibby and Beatrice de Cardi, and the Danish ethnographer Klaus Ferdinand, whose work on recording the traditional way of life of the bedouin will always be remembered with gratitude by the people of Qatar.

There are still comparatively few publications available for the visitor or expatriate resident who wishes to know more of this country. This, then, is the book I would have liked to have had when I first came to Qatar.

Acknowledgements

Many people have contributed to this book, helping to track down and verify information, freely lending me their photographs, and providing kind encouragement. My greatest debt is to my husband David, who has supported all my endeavours over the years, is the driver and navigator on our weekend desert expeditions, and has taken many photographs specially for the book. Marijcke Jongbloed's many publications on the flora and fauna of the UAE first inspired me with the idea that one day I might attempt something of the sort myself. She encouraged me to go ahead, neither of us realising at the time that her support would eventually extend to her editing and publishing the book! She has also supplied many of the photographs.

The staff of the Centre for Geographic Information Systems, Qatar, were most helpful in creating a map to my own specifications, and lending photographs. Mohammed al Bloshi, Director of the Department of Museums and Antiquities, The National Council for Culture, Arts and Heritage, kindly assisted me in locating some early photographs of Qatar and arranged for them to be made available. Prof. Dionisius Agius of the University of Leeds and Shirley Kay, an archaeologist and writer formerly resident in Bahrain and the UAE, generously allowed me to use photographs of theirs which had appeared in their own publications. Dr Sibba Einarsdottir, Curator of the Ethnographic Collections at Moesgaard Museum in Denmark, spent much time selecting and sending photographs taken by my late friend Klaus Ferdinand and his colleague Jette Bang during the months they spent with the bedouin people of Qatar in 1959.

Dr Henning Schwarz, who was with me on a UNESCO expedition to the Hawar Islands in 2003, kindly sent me some of his pictures of ospreys and cormorants taken on that occasion, and Dennis Johnson, who has photographed ospreys all over the world, also loaned me pictures. Dr Nick Pilcher, an internationally recognised consultant on the conservation of sea turtles and a frequent visitor to Qatar, sent me two hundred of his photographs to choose from, so that it was hard to make the small selection which appear in this book! Dr Robert Baldwin, a marine consultant resident in Oman, and Dr Drew Gardner of Zayed University, Abu Dhabi, both gave me much enthusiastic encouragement and supplied me with many of their superb pictures.

To all these friends, and to all the members of the Qatar Natural History Group who kept asking, 'When are you going to write a book on Qatar?' my thanks.

Last but not least, publication of this book would not have been possible without the generous sponsorship of Rasgas Company Ltd., for which I am deeply grateful.

The author holding Amal, the youngest addition to a family of the Al Murrah

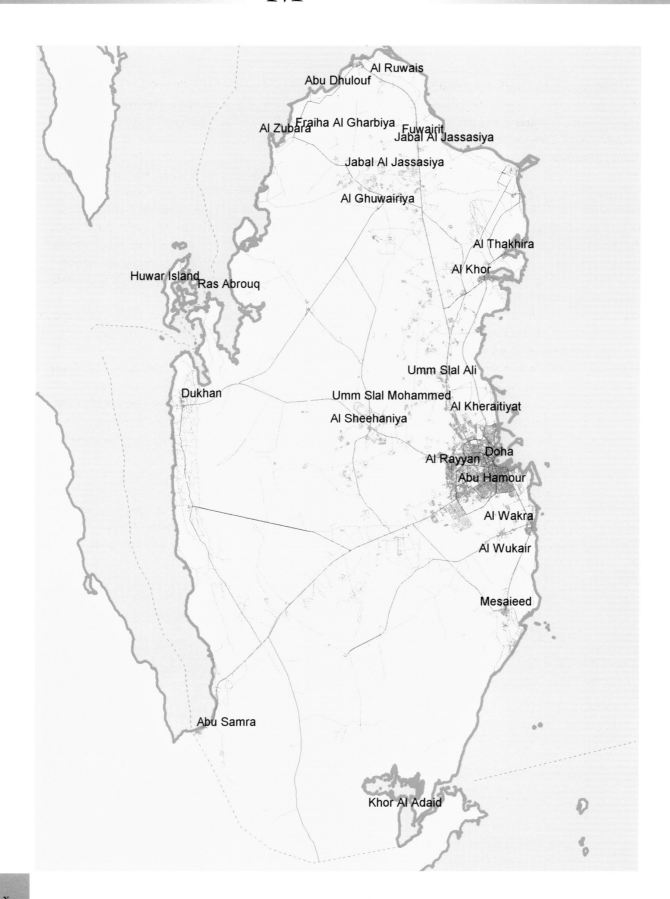

THE LAND

HALFWAY ALONG THE WESTERN COAST OF THE ARABIAN GULF LIES THE SMALL PENINSULA of Qatar, extending almost 180 kilometres northwards into the warm, shallow seas of the Arabian Gulf. Appropriately, as Qatar is one of the world's leading producers of oil and gas, its 11,437 square kilometres resemble an oil-flare in shape.

From the air the impression is of a predominantly flat terrain, with colours ranging from the golden-brown of the arid desert to the pale cream of the coastal salt-flats (*sabkha*), patched here and there with the vivid green of farms and date-palm plantations. On three sides it is surrounded by the sea, which runs through a spectrum of colours from a brilliant blue-green to a deep indigo blue, with the yellow of shoals and sand banks dotted around the coast. To the south it shares a border with Saudi Arabia. So narrow is the base of the peninsula that it used to be said that three men strategically placed could watch the whole border from coast to coast. Qatar has less than 5 inches of rain per year and summer temperatures are searing hot, but in the winter months the north wind blows continuously and despite the almost constant sunshine the temperature is pleasantly cool.

Once on the ground the visitor's first impression of uniform flatness is quickly modified, as the landscape of Qatar is surprisingly varied, given its modest size. With no rivers and little rainfall, it has been shaped only by the forces of wind and sea.

There are several distinct regions. The highest point is a hill in the south-west of 103 metres, and bordering the western coast-line at Ras Abrouq are lofty plateaux of gleaming white soft limestone, topped with a harder layer, also of limestone. Over aeons of time, windblown sand has scoured and honed the edges of the platforms into weird shapes: spindly pinnacles and free-standing giant mushrooms. Green forests of mangroves fringe the north-eastern coast, while patches of sparse vegetation are found on the rolling central gravel plains.

In the south the coastal salt-flats give way to one of the most spectacular landscapes in the entire Gulf region: majestic dunes of fine golden sand, varying from crescent-shaped *barchans*, 50 metres in height, to the long, undulating ridges known as *seif* dunes. Driven by the prevailing north-westerly wind, the *shamal*, the dunes drift steadily down to Khor al Adaid, a tidal lagoon which marks the southern border of Qatar. In time, as the dunes continue their slow march southwards ahead of the wind, this stretch of water will disappear beneath the sands.

Landscape at the inland sea, Khor al Adaid

THE GEOLOGY

Deep within the earth lie the massive deposits of hydrocarbons which have transformed Qatar in under a century from a sparsely-populated country whose principal income came from pearl-fishing to one of the world's largest suppliers of energy and the richest nation, per capita, on earth. However, there is little evidence at the surface for the source of this vast wealth, other than the elongated Dukhan dome. This is the surface expression of the structure that trapped the oil-yielding marine sediments in the Jurassic and Cretaceous strata some 250 million years ago.

With the exception of the Dukhan dome, the oldest surface rocks of Qatar are the comparatively youthful limestones of the Middle Eocene period of 48 to 45 million years ago. Salts within the limestone have precipitated, through evaporation, to become 'gypsum', providing material for the finely-carved decorative facings on traditional buildings. Caves and depressions were formed in the 'karst' limestone by the dissolution of the evaporates by rainwater, the most spectacular being the large cave known as Dahl al Misfir, the Cave of Brightness, south-west of Doha. Present-day oases are found in some of the depressions.

Dahl al Misfir

Also from the Middle Eocene period date the Midra shales containing sharks' teeth and other marine fossils, for at this time the land that was to become Qatar lay under water, and all kinds of sea creatures swam over what is now sun-baked desert. The sea level was to rise and fall many times over the millennia. Many inland *sabkhas* were shallow marine entrapments as recently as 8000 years ago and today seashells lie scattered on the desert floor, far from the sea. Eager amateur naturalists hunt for marine fossils in the deposits along the western and eastern coasts.

In the hills bordering the Bay of Salwa in the far south-west the spectacular gypsum pavements of the following Miocene period are to be found, composed of radiating rings of glittering crystalline slabs. During this period a gradual lifting of the land raised parts of it above sealevel.

Gypsum pavements

Five million years ago a great river flowing from Eastern Arabia deposited a blanket of river gravel over much of central and eastern Qatar. Some of these many-coloured, smooth pebbles were rolled and shaped by the wind to form the curious three-faceted stones known to geologists as *'ventifacts'* or *'dreikanters'*.

During the Pleistocene period of approximately 2,000,000 years ago successive ice ages, confining much of the earth's of the earth's water in the polar ice caps, caused a global drop in sealevels. The Arabian Gulf became dry between about 70,000 and 44,000 years ago. Repeatedly re-flooding between the ice ages, it became dry again about 15,000 years ago. Winds blew sand from the bed of the Gulf onto the land to form tall dunes, along with the thin layer of powdery reddish topsoil which supports the desert vegetation of today.

THE FIRST SIGNS OF MAN

When humans first migrated into Qatar, they found a terrain whose lack of surface water did not encourage permanent settlement. It may be that during a period when the Gulf was dry the earliest hunter-gatherers crossed the marshy ground from what is now Iran and reached the eastern borders of the Arabian landmass, but no trace of their passing has yet been discovered. It is only in the last thirty years that a late date for human occupation of eastern Arabia has been widely accepted. Excavations at Al Khor on the east coast by the French mission from 1976 onwards proved, by means of carbon dating, that what had previously been assumed to be different cultures from widely differing periods could all be dated to between 5600 and 5300 BC. Al Shagra, the remains of a fishing settlement in the south-east, is Qatar's most ancient archaeological site at c.6000 BC.

Hunters and fishermen set up camps along the shores of the eastern and western coast, trapping birds and preying on gazelle, onager (a species of wild ass) and hares. Besides fish, the sea yielded dugongs and turtles. Higher rainfall 7000 years ago resulted in shallow freshwater stands forming on the west coast near what is now Umm Bab. There is evidence that fish were caught and dried, perhaps for trading. Few traces of the hunter-gatherers' shelters remain, but many of their stone tools still lie upon the desert surface where they were abandoned so long ago. Among them are some of the most beautiful ever produced by any Stone Age peoples.
Besides hunting and fishing, ancient Qataris gathered wild cereals and ground them into meal in stone querns. The presence on half a dozen sites of shards of thin pottery with painted decoration in red and brown, known as Al Ubaid (after the site of its manufacture in Iraq), suggests that people were trading with inhabitants of other lands. Rich deposits of first-grade flint in Qatar enabled the export of 'blanks' – roughly shaped tools that could be precision-finished later – down the coast to what is now the UAE.

Clay tablets with written records have been discovered in Mesopotamia, in what is now modern Iraq, providing evidence of long trading voyages taking place along the Arabian peninsula as early as the fourth millennium BC. The Sumerians of Mesopotamia had established the world's earliest city-states in the fertile plain between the Tigris and

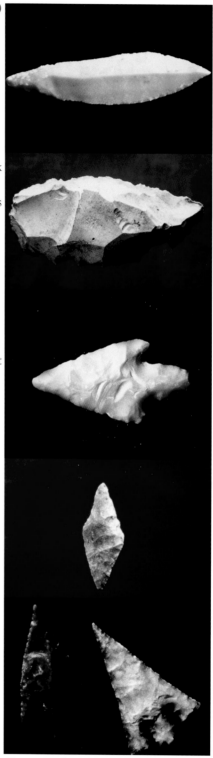

From top to bottom:
Blade arrowhead, scraper, tanged and barbed arrowhead, diamond-shaped arrowhead, tanged and barbed arrowheads.

3

Euphrates rivers. Inscriptions refer to trade with the land of Dilmun, which included the whole eastern coast of Arabia. The Sumerian states traded textiles, silver jewellery and oil in exchange for copper, timber and hard stone for building.

Channelled through the Gulf, the trade resulted in Bronze Age civilisations springing up and flourishing along both coasts. From 2450 to 1700 BC Dilmun was centred in Bahrain. That Qatar played a part in the trading network is evident from the presence of fine red 'Barbar' pottery with a ridged decoration, which was manufactured in Bahrain. It is named after a site where large quantities of it have been found, the Barbar Temple near the modern village of Barbar in the north of Bahrain. This pottery has been found in a depression on the Ras Abrouq peninsula on the west coast of Qatar and on a small island in the eastern bay of Khor Shaqiq.

By around 1700 BC the power-base in the region shifted, as southern Mesopotamia, which had previously imported materials mainly from the east and south-east, reoriented towards the north and west. The Kassites, a northern people from the Zagros mountains, had assumed power in the middle of the second millennium, and Dilmun gradually became part of Kassite Babylonia.

There is little evidence for human occupation of Qatar at this period, but one unique site, dating to around 1400 BC, exists on the small island in the bay of Al Khor. Here, middens contain the crushed remains of millions of shells of a sea-snail, *Thais savignyi*. This shellfish yields a scarlet dye, and the island is the first dye-producing site to have been found in the Arabian Gulf. Scarlet and purple-dyed cloth was much in demand for clothes worn by the elite in Kassite Babylonia. Besides producing the valuable dye, people living on the peninsula of Qatar participated in the pearl trade since very ancient times.

Kassite potsherds and shells of Thais savignyi, Jazirat bin Ghanim

Camels had been domesticated as far back as the third millennium, probably first as milk animals and later as beasts of burden. By the Iron Age some of the inhabitants of Qatar may have become nomadic pastoralists, the ancestors of the bedouin, herding goats and sheep besides camels. The climate was now drier than in the Neolithic period.

MORE RECENT HISTORY

By the 6th century BC settlers and nomads had become interdependent, exchanging commodities and using camels for overland trade, augmenting the traditional sea-routes. Herodotus, a Greek historian writing in the 5th century BC said that the inhabitants of this region were excellent sailors and good tradesmen.

In the 1st century BC the Roman writer Pliny the Elder refers to the nomadic people of the region as 'Catharrei', and in the 2nd century AD the writer Ptolemy recorded 'Catarra' on a map of Arabia.

In 326 BC Alexander the Great conquered Persia. Invading the Indian sub-continent, he had a large fleet of ships constructed near present-day Karachi. He then sent his admiral, Nearchos the Cretan, to explore the coast of Arabia. Nearchos entered the Arabian Gulf at Ras Musandam, but Alexander's untimely death, three days before the planned campaign to conquer Arabia, ended the attempt. The vast empire of Alexander was divided among his generals. The eastern region was taken by Seleukos Nictator, who established his capital at Seleucia on the west bank of the Tigris. The city of Gerrha, on the coast of Arabia north of Qatar, became a centre for trade between India and Arabia by both land and sea. Pottery fragments from this period, known as Seleucid ware, have been found at Ras Uwainat Ali on Qatar's west coast. A nearby scattering of burial mounds on the small peninsula of Ras Abaruk has been provisionally dated to this period, as well as a fish-processing complex on the same peninsula.

The Parthians, a Persian people, rose to power around 140 BC and began to interrupt the Graeco-Roman trading routes between Europe and Asia via the Arabian Gulf, so that the routes shifted to the Red Sea. In 225 AD the Parthians were overthrown and the Sassanid dynasty was established. Their capital was established at Ctesiphon in Iraq and trade routes reverted to the Gulf and the Indian Ocean. These routes over land and sea were, of course, arteries not only of trade, but were instrumental in the dissemination of knowledge and in spreading cultural influence.

It is likely that pearls and the red dye obtained from shellfish continued to be exported from Qatar during the Sassanid period. At Al Mazrouah, north-west of Doha, a burial mound contained two skeletons, one of a tall male with an iron arrowhead still embedded in a bone of his forearm. Arrowheads and a sword of iron and an almost intact Sassanian glass lay beside the warrior. Around the grave were the remains of camels. Near Umm-Al-Ma on the north-west coast a small settlement has been excavated from this period: it contained fragments of glass and pottery including Sassanian-Islamic glazed ware. Finds like these indicate that the standard of living of the villagers was well above subsistence level.

Umm-al-Ma: above: grave with skeleton, below: burial grounds

In the early centuries AD it seems likely that small settlements of Nestorian Christians existed in Qatar, as there is a reference to a synod of bishops meeting in the country. Ancient churches have been excavated on Failaka island off Kuwait, at Jumail in Saudi Arabia, and on the island of Sir Bani Yas in Abu Dhabi. The Christian communities presumably existed alongside their pagan neighbours.

The call to embrace Islam came in 627-629. The new faith was adopted by the Christian governor of Hasa Oasis in the eastern province of Saudi Arabia. Others followed, and the new ideology, which taught the

equality and brotherhood of all Muslims, introduced an era of exploration and expansion. By the end of the seventh century Islam had spread throughout the whole of the Arabian peninsula. The Abbasids, who were descended from the uncle of the Prophet, overthrew the Ummayid dynasty, centred in Damascus, in 750. This ushered in a golden age of trade in the Arabian Gulf that spanned two centuries. The Abbasids set up their capital in Baghdad and constructed the port of Basra at the mouth of the Euphrates and Tigris to handle the vast range of goods pouring into the region. Tang china found at widespread Gulf sites is evidence of well-established trade with China. China exported spices, musk, camphor and silk to the Abbasids, who sent garments of cotton and wool and a variety of metal goods. Besides the exchange of commodities with China, trade with India and East Africa increased, and Suhar in Oman became an important port.

Little is known about Qatar in this period, but undoubtedly the local pearling industry benefited from the demand for pearls in Abbasid Baghdad. Two Arab geographers of the 10th century mention Qatar, and there is a reference by the geographer Yaqut al Hamawi, who died in 1229, to the export of red woollen cloaks from Qatar. He also mentions the renowned markets for horses and camels. One such market may well have existed at Murwab, a town south of Al Zubara, which dates to the 9th to 11th centuries. It is the only sizeable ancient settlement in Qatar not located on the coast. Some 250 houses, a fort and two mosques have been excavated. The fort is the oldest yet discovered in Qatar and is of a style similar to forts in Iraq of the eighth to eleventh centuries. Remains of fine quality ceramics and glassware are an indication of the affluence of the inhabitants.

The island of Hormuz at the mouth of the Gulf became important as a maritime power, and gained increasing control over trade in the region. But in 1515 Hormuz was taken by the Portuguese admiral Albuquerque. Bahrain fell to the Portuguese shortly afterwards, followed by other Gulf ports. Maritime traffic in the Gulf remained under Portuguese control for almost a century. Meanwhile, north of the Gulf the Ottoman Turks occupied Basra and made several attempts to oust the Portuguese from their strongholds. This was finally achieved by Shah Abbas of Persia, who allied with the English and took Hormuz from the Portuguese in 1622. In 1650 they were finally expelled from Muscat. The English East India Company was formed in 1600 and its Dutch counterpart two years later, and for most of the seventeenth century Gulf trade was dominated by 'merchant adventurers' from England, Holland and later, France. Qatar played little part in these struggles for domination, having too few natural resources to attract the cupidity of conquerors. The central plains were the domain of the bedouin (*badu*) tribes with their herds of camels and flocks of sheep and goats, constantly moving in search of

Glazed water jar found at Al Murwab

fresh pastures. The settled people of the coast (*hadar*) continued with the immemorial activities of pearling, trading and fishing. Al Huwaila on the north-east coast developed as the principal pearling port in the early 18th century, to be superceded in the later part of the century by Al Zubara in the north-west. Other settlements of the time were at Al Wakra, Al Ghuwairiyah and Al Bidda, the village which was one day to become Al Doha, the capital.

Al Zubara developed around 1760 when members of the Utub clan migrated there from Kuwait, and it quickly became an important centre for trade and pearling. In 1766 Basra fell to the Persians and many of its inhabitants moved to Al Zubara. Al Murair fort was built in 1768 to protect Al Zubara from land attack, and the following year a two-kilometre-long canal was constructed between the sea and the fort. A wall was constructed around the settlement, and enlarged when the population expanded in the nineteenth century. A colourful figure from this period is Rahmah bin Jabir. A member of the Jalahaimah branch of the Utub, he became a lifelong enemy of the Al Khalifah, another branch who had settled in Bahrain. He established his base in Khor Hassan, a few miles north of Al Zubara. For the next half century the history of Qatar was dominated by his vendetta against the Al Khalifah. He attacked the ships of the Ottoman empire, Kuwait, Bahrain and Persia, on one occasion capturing a fleet of 20 *battils* enroute from Kuwait to Muscat. He was careful, however, not to incur the enmity of the British. By 1800 Rahmah had become the most powerful tribal leader in Qatar. Over the next few years he captured 18 cargo vessels belonging to the Utub. Then Omani attacks on Bahrain and Qatar forced him to remove to Dammam in al Hasa, from where he renewed his seafaring activities against the Al Khalifah. When his stronghold in Dammam was blown up by Saudi forces, Rahmah, together with 500 families of his followers, removed to Bushire. Returning to Dammam in 1818, he continued his attacks on the ships of those he regarded as his enemies, finally agreeing reluctantly to a declaration of peace in 1824. The peace proved short-lived. In 1826, in battle with an Utub fleet, he blew up

Goats grazing under palm trees at Sheehaniya

7

his own ship with himself and his eight-year-old son on board, rather than face defeat. A British official of the time described the formidable appearance of the old man in his last days, his arms, legs and head covered with the scars of battle.

The British were concerned that fighting among the Gulf tribal rulers could disrupt their trade with India, and in 1820 they persuaded the ruling sheikhs to agree to a General Treaty of Peace. A Maritime Truce, formulated by the British, took effect from 1832, outlawing warfare during the pearling season from May to November.

Around this time Sheikh Mohammed bin Thani Al-Thani became the most influential leader in Qatar. The family stemmed from the Bani Tamim and the Al-Maadhid of central Arabia. It was with Sheikh Mohammed that the British political agent, Col. Pelly, negotiated a new treaty in 1868. As a result of this pact Sheikh Mohammed agreed not to make war at sea and to allow the British to act as negotiators in settling any quarrels that might arise between Bahrain and Qatar. Through skilful leadership the whole peninsula of Qatar gradually came under the control of the Al-Thani family.

Donkeys carrying water in leather containers from a well on the outskirts of Doha, 1950's

View of the waterfront of Doha showing the Diwan Emiri in the centre, 1958

The influence of the Ottoman Turks gradually expanded in the second half of the 19th century, and in 1872 a hundred Ottoman troops landed at Al Bidda (the former name of the capital, Al Doha) and established themselves in a fort. It was alleged that the troops had been sent in response to the harassment of the town-dwellers by bedouin tribesmen. The Ottoman presence continued in Qatar for around 40 years, reluctantly tolerated by the population. In 1893 on the occasion of the visit to Al Bidda by Nafiz Pasha, the Wali of Basra, matters came to a head. After an attempted surprise attack on Sheikh Jassim bin Mohammed Al-Thani at night in his fort at Al Wajba, west of Al Bidda, he successfully routed the Ottoman forces in battle. This victory marked a watershed in the history of Qatar, not only in the reinforcement of Al-Thani rule but in strengthening the concept held by Qataris of themselves as citizens of an independent state. Ottoman influence waned, and during the First World War the last remaining Ottoman troops withdrew from Qatar.

In 1916 the Ruler of Qatar, Sheikh Jassim's son Sheikh Abdullah, who had succeeded him in 1913, signed the Anglo-Qatar Treaty. Sheikh Abdullah agreed not to have relations with any foreign power without British consent, to admit British subjects to Qatar, and to allow the establishment of post and telegraph services. In return, Britain promised to protect Qatar in the event of attack by land or sea.

The 1930s were years of severe economic hardship for Qatar. The recession affecting the western world caused the demand for pearls to fall. In 1933 the development of the cultured pearl by the Japanese dealt a crippling blow to the Gulf pearl industry, from which it never recovered. Many families emigrated and those that remained struggled to survive.

THE OIL ERA

At this bleak time, new hope appeared. The possibility of the existence of oil in the Gulf region had been realised as early as 1908, but for many years little effort had been made to prospect for oil in the southern Gulf. Then, in 1932, the American oil company Socal struck oil in Bahrain. Socal had offered the ruler of Saudi Arabia very attractive terms, but in Qatar the British managed to convince Sheikh Abdullah that he

Persian water-carrier (Kandari), Al Jaara area of Doha, 1950's

should accept the more modest offer made by the British-controlled Iraq Petroleum Company.

Oil was discovered in Qatar in 1939, but World War II brought a halt to the planned production. It was not until 1949 that exploitation of the country's enormous oil reserves began. No one at that time could have imagined their extent or the extent of the wealth that would transform Qatar and its people.

Within two decades of the first production of oil the country developed rapidly. Education was a priority and in 1956 the state education system was set up. The University of Qatar opened in 1973.

Women began to play an ever-increasing part in decision-making at a national level and in the workplace. In 2003 a woman was appointed as Minister of Education, the first in the Gulf region. Heading the educational revolution is the Qatar Foundation for Education, Science and Community Development, set up in 1995 and chaired by Sheikha Mozah bint Nasser Al Misned, the consort of H.H. the Emir and mother of the Heir Apparent Sheikh Tamim bin Hamad bin Khalifa Al-Thani. The aim of the Foundation is to provide the highest standards of education for future citizens. Education City has been established on the historic site where Sheikh Jassim bin Mohammed al-Thani defeated the Ottoman forces in 1893. It houses Qatar Academy, a Learning Centre for

In 1944 Sheikh Abdullah retired from active government and handed over to his son Sheikh Hamad. Sheikh Hamad, who suffered from ill health, died in 1948, and his brother Sheikh Ali became the Ruler in 1949 when old Sheikh Abdullah formally abdicated. On Sheikh Ali's abdication in 1960 his son Sheikh Ahmed came to power. In 1971 Qatar became independent of Britain's protectorate role, and the following year Sheikh Khalifa bin Hamad assumed power from his cousin. In 1995 H.H. Sheikh Hamad bin Khalifa Al-Thani took over the rule of the country from his father.

The Museum of Islamic Art under construction on the Doha corniche

Four Seasons Hotel, Doha

children with special needs, and branch campuses of some of the world's leading universities. Several hospitals were built during the 1960s, with the state-of-the-art Hamad General Hospital opening in Al Doha in 1982.

In the 1970s the discovery of the North Dome Gas Field began the switch from an oil-based to a gas-based economy. Still, many years of development were needed before the shipments of Liquefied Natural Gas began to flow regularly from Ras Laffan to the Far East.

In the last decade, Qatar has seen more rapid development than at any previous period in its history. In 1996 the world's best-known Arabic news channel, Al Jazeera, was founded. With 50 million viewers worldwide and rapidly expanding, Al Jazeera has helped to make the name of Qatar famous. Al Jazeera International planned to begin broadcasting in English in 2006.

The capital of Qatar, Al Doha, has expanded to become a well-laid-out city around the shores of the bay of Al Doha. Its skyline changes month by month, as more and more high-rise buildings are constructed. North of the bay a massive offshore holiday and residential development, The Pearl, is under construction. The whole country is gearing up for the hosting of the Asian Games in December 2006, with the upgrading of road networks as well as the construction of purpose-built sports venues and accommodation for thousands of athletes. With a *per capita* income forecast to be among the highest in the world, Qatari citizens have every reason to look forward to the future with confidence.

THE COLOUR PURPLE

Flamingoes wade in the shallows

A LITTLE ISLAND, WITH FINE GOLDEN SANDS AND LOW, GLEAMING white limestone cliffs, lies in a wide bay, close within the curving embrace of the nearby mainland. The sparkling water is jade green in the shallows and merges into a soft aquamarine where the natural channels lie. Surrounding the island is a forest of green, salt-encrusted mangroves, the home of countless birds. Jewelled king-fishers flash by, and purple herons, pink flamingoes and glossy ibis wade in the shallows. Their strange, haunting calls echo over the island. Over all arches the deep and infinite blue of the sky.

A peaceful scene, rich in natural hues. But no colour is so intense as that over which a huddle of brown-skinned men are toiling on the sandy shores of the island. In front of a group of small stone-walled hovels, roofs roughly thatched with palm fronds, are large vats made of coarse, thick, green-coloured clay. Steam rises as the contents of the vats simmer over deep pits of glowing charcoal. Within each pot a hellish brew is boiling. The stench of rotten fish is nauseating. More than once a worker turns away to retch. The viscous red liquid bubbles and steams. The men's hands are red to the wrists, their garments splashed with scarlet. Their brows seem to be smeared with blood as they pause, now and again, to wipe away the sweat with the back of a hand.

Scenes very like this actually happened in Qatar more than three thousand years ago. On a small island in the bay of Khor Shaqiq an industry was set up to supply one of the most valuable of ancient commodities - one that was more precious than gold. The rich, purple-red dye produced from a species of sea snail was used only for the robes of kings and the elite few whom they chose to honour. Red, the colour of blood, of fire, of the sun and therefore of life itself, was seen in many ancient societies as a symbol of power and strength. It is not difficult to understand how a man wearing garments of purple or red became a symbol of power, particularly if the use of the colour was confined to the ruler and his immediate associates. Even today we associate purple and red with authority, in expressions such as 'born to wear the purple', and 'purple airway' – air traffic controllers' jargon for a route reserved for an aircraft carrying royalty!

The dyes produced from sea snails ranged from a deep bluish-purple to the most brilliant scarlet, depending on the species used and the method of preparation. In the languages of the ancient peoples who made the dyes, there is no clear distinction between purple and red; they are interchangeable. The earliest manufacturers of shellfish dyes were almost certainly the Phoenicians, a Mediterranean people originating in Lebanon. They are sometimes referred to as Canaanites, but the Greeks called them *phoinikes* – the red people — because of the red cloth they exported. From the 9th to the 6th centuries BC they dominated trade in the Mediterranean, establishing colonies in Cyprus, Greece, Italy, Spain and N Africa. One of the great Phoenician cities in Lebanon, Tyre, was the home of the dye industry, which began around 1600 BC. But dye was produced all over the Phoenician empire. At Tarentum in Italy there is a small hill composed entirely of the remains of murex shells.

A Phoenician legend recounts the discovery of the purple dye. The god Melkarth was strolling along the beach with his sheep-dog one day when the animal crunched on a shellfish. Noticing the dog's jaws stained with red, the god realised its significance. He had a gown made from wool dyed in the new colour and presented it to his girlfriend, the nymph Tyros, thus starting a fashion trend which has lasted more than three thousand years.

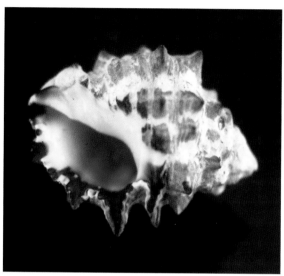

Thais savignyi shell, 40 mm in length

The most commonly used sea snails were *Murex trunculus*, which yields a bluish-purple colour, and *Murex brandaris* which gives a red-purple. The dye is released when the hyperbranchial gland in the animal is crushed and reacts with a naturally present enzyme. In the case of *Murex trunculus* the presence of light is also necessary for the colour to develop, but not in the case of *Murex brandaris*. Many other species of sea snails yield the dye, among them *Murex tribulus,* still widely eaten in Spain today, as well as *Thais purpura haemastoma* and, on the little island off the coast of Qatar, *Thais savignyi.*

The Roman writer Pliny, writing in 70 AD, has left us a detailed description of the dye-extraction process. The shellfish were harvested in the winter months. Murex are carnivores, living at depths of 5 to 15 metres and feeding on other shellfish by boring holes in their shells. According to Pliny, the shell-fishers used to lower baskets of shellfish bait, wait for murex to gather on them, and then quickly draw them up. The murex were then kept alive in tanks until a sufficient quantity had been gathered and dye production could begin. Ancient writers state that the dyers' hands were permanently stained red, and that the stench from centres of the trade, such as Tyre, was formidable!

He says that the smaller shellfish (*Murex trunculus*) were crushed, shell and all, whereas the larger ones (*Murex brandaris*) were pierced and the hyperbranchial gland extracted. The crushed mass was macerated in heavily salted water for three days. This may have been to suppress the bacterial content of the vats, as the bacteria produced by rotten fish (*Clostridium carnis*) are highly dangerous. The rotting shellfish were then rinsed thoroughly and boiled for ten days until reduced to a sixteenth of the original amount. Testing by dipping wool then began and boiling continued until the dye had reached the desired degree of brilliance.

Wool was always dyed in the strand, never in the cloth. So valuable and expensive was the genuine dye, which retained its brilliant hues without fading, that in classical antiquity a whole industry sprang up, forging purple dyes using cheaper materials. Among them were flowers such as mulberry blossoms and amaranth, and the roots of plants, and the dyes had to be fixed using additions of ferro-acetate, laurel, cantharidae or haematite. A lustre could be imparted to the thread by adding gall-nuts or iris roots to the mixture. A document in demotic Greek known as the Stockholm papyrus, found in a grave in Egypt of the third century AD, actually lists as many as seventy recipes for these dyes, and its author claimed, with evident satisfaction, that it was impossible to distinguish the counterfeit from the original purple. The headquarters of the counterfeit dye production was Egypt.

There are countless references to the wearing of purple in ancient literature. Only the Roman emperors and senior imperial officials could have a purple border on their togas. The Achaemenian kings of Persia wore purple: Darius the Mede advanced in state to meet Alexander the Great wearing a robe of purple and white. And when Alexander conquered the Persian capital, Susa, in 331 BC he found 200-year-old purple robes in the royal treasury that glowed as brightly as the day they were woven. Alexander himself adopted the Persian custom of wearing purple and his generals also sported purple cloaks.

In Babylonia, a region in what is now Iraq, a mountain people called the Kassites invaded and took control of the country soon after 1595 BC, and the next three centuries saw a period of great economic prosperity in the region. Production of purple dye on Jazirat bin Ghanim (Al Khor island) in Qatar occurred as part of the take-over of the Dilmun trading civilisation by the Kassites between 1425 and 1225 BC. The Dilmun trading empire included the islands and mainland between Kuwait and Bahrain. In the early 1980s an American archaeologist, Christopher Edens, working with the 'Mission Française Archéologique à Qatar', excavated a site on the island. The remains of pottery enabled it to be dated to around 1400 BC.

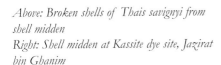

Above: Broken shells of Thais savignyi from shell midden
Right: Shell midden at Kassite dye site, Jazirat bin Ghanim

It consisted of about five rectangular structures, several hearths and stone kists. One pit contained the remains of around 38,000 shellfish, a species called *Thais savignyi*. There was also a huge shell midden measuring 10 by 15 metres. The top layer consisted of food remains — shells and fish bones and debris from hearths — but as the archaeologists dug down they came upon a deep, solid layer of shells of *Thais savignyi*. This shellfish, which lives under rocks in the intertidal zone, produces a bright red dye. It requires light plus an enzyme to release the dye from the hyperbranchial gland.

The archaeologists calculated, to their astonishment, that the mound they had excavated contained the remains of almost 3 million shellfish! There were other mounds that appeared to contain similar quantities. The archaeologists conducted experiments collecting the shellfish. They concluded that collecting 3 million snails would have taken 42,000 man-hours of labour: 20 people working one month a year for 7 years. There was only one possible conclusion: the site had been used for dye production. It was unique -

the first site of its kind in the entire Arabian Gulf and the only one found outside the Mediterranean. The pottery found on the site, which included the remains of huge, thick-walled vats, was clearly Kassite. Evidently the dye was being produced for use in Babylonia. The Kassites were a literate people. Their records mention that their kings wore red-purple garments and gave gifts of the same to political supporters and senior officials. The red cloth was often presented in combination with linen and gold.

So who were the shell-gatherers, the men who toiled in wretched conditions to produce this rare commodity? Were they local tribesmen, or slaves of the Kassites, or even Kassites themselves? We will never know. They left no graves, no trace of themselves save the few remains that gave clues as to the nature of their activities. No source of fresh water has been found on the island, so they probably had to bring supplies across from the nearby mainland. Pearl fishing was undoubtedly being carried out in Qatar at this time, possibly even from the same island. It is indeed ironic that the men who laboured to supply two of the most beautiful and expensive luxuries of ancient times themselves lived the simplest and harshest of lives.

Excavated remains of buildings on the Kassite dye site, Jazirat bin Ghanim

CUP-MARKED ROCKS OF AL JASSASIYA

AROUND THE COASTS OF QATAR, AND AT TWO SITES ON JAZIRAT AL HUWAR LOCATED to the north-west of the peninsula, are low limestone hills (*jebel*) bearing numbers of cup-marks cut into the rock. Some of these small, circular depressions are single; others are massed together in a wide variety of formations: one, two, three or four lines of cups, sometimes straight and sometimes curved, or clustered together in 'rosettes' with anything from six to sixteen cups surrounding a central depression. The southern-most of these hills is Jebel Al Wakra (now enclosed by a security fence and inaccessible to visitors) to the south of Doha. At Jebel Al Jassasiya, an hour's drive to the north, can be seen the greatest number of carvings anywhere in the country. A short distance north lies Jebel Fuwairit, also with numerous cup-marks, and isolated carvings occur on small, scattered limestone mounds around the northern coast leading down to the second major petroglyph site, a line of limestone *jebel* outcrops between Fraiha Al Gharbiya and Zubara in the north-west.

The Danish archaeologist Holger Kapel and his son Hans surveyed and drew the carvings at Jebel Al Jassasiya in 1974, and in 1984 a consultant working at Hamad Hospital, Professor D F Hawkins, carried out a similar careful study at Jebel Al Fraiha. A Middle Eastern historian, William Facey, published a monograph on the Jebel Al Jassasiya petroglyphs in 1987.

In 1882, commenting on remarkably similar rows of cup marks which occur on rocks in Scotland, a historian remarked, 'Whatever may have been their motive, the cup markers showed a decided liking for arranging their sculpturing in regularly shaped rows.' At Jebel Al Jassasiya, of the 874 carvings recorded by the Kapels in 1974, 333 consist of cupmarks in rows.

Both Kapel and Hawkins considered that the parallel rows of cup-marks were used for playing the ancient board game known to archaeologists as the '*mancala*' game, because that happened to be the African name under which it was first recorded by Europeans. Rather touchingly, Kapel imagines fishermen and merchants sitting on the *jebel* watching for the boats to come in and whiling away the time playing games. It is an attractive picture.

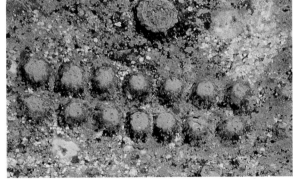

'Mancala' game

Before going on to consider the drawbacks to this theory, it is worth taking a look at the game itself.

It is easy to make a cup-mark on a horizontal limestone surface using basic tools. A lump of flint placed on the rock and hit with a hammer soon leaves a depression in the soft stone. When a sufficiently deep indentation has been made, the inside can be scoured and smoothed with the sharp edge of a piece of flint. The *mancala* game is of immense antiquity. Several boards have been found carved into the stone surfaces of Khurna temple at Thebes in Egypt, which dates back to 1400 BC. It occurs all over the Arabian Gulf from Kuwait to Oman and also in Iran, although Qatar is unique in the sheer quantities of its carvings. In some parts of Arabia it went by the name of *Al Huwais*, and in Qatar it was known as *Al Haloosa* or *Al Huwaila*. The game is found in almost every African country, where it appears under countless names. It may well have been introduced into Africa by the Arabs. From Africa the slave-trade took the game to Cuba. In India and Malaya two of its names are *Narani* and *Chanka*. The number of holes and rows of holes and the number of counters used vary considerably from country to country, but the basic principle of the game is the same throughout.

In a version recorded in Kuwait, two players sit, one on each side of the board, and place their counters into the row of holes on their side, dividing them equally between the holes. Small pebbles or seeds are usually used as counters. Each player in turn removes the counters from a hole in his own row, selected at random, and drops them consecutively one by one into other holes, starting to the immediate right of the emptied hole. On reaching the last hole in the row, he continues to deposit the counters into his opponent's holes. The second player then does the same. Often a large number of counters may accumulate in one cup: a player may check on the number of counters in one of his own holes but not in his opponent's. As the game proceeds, if the hole in which a player places his last counter is on his opponent's side and contains, after the addition, either 2 or 3 counters he may 'capture' and remove them, and may also do the same with counters from the consecutively preceding cups on his opponent's side if they contain either 2 or 3 counters. The skill of the game lies in the player rapidly calculating from which of his holes to move the counters in order to capture as many as possible of his opponent's. The game continues until one opponent cannot move

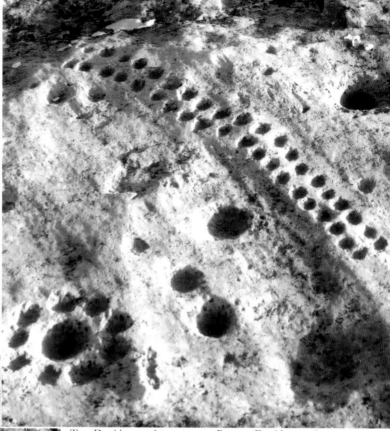

Top: Double row of twenty cups. Bottom: Double row of seven cups. Right: Double row of cupmarks

or until there is no possibility of further capture. The player with the greatest number of captured counters is the winner.

In addition to the game boards on the *jebel* are the 'rosettes', with numbers of shallow holes arranged in a circle around a central hole. This is said to be a game known as Al Aila in Qatar and Um Al Judaira in Kuwait, Bahrain and Oman. At Jebel Al Jassasiya Holger Kapel recorded a total of 333 game boards, of which 193 had two rows each of even holes. Seventy-one rosettes were recorded, of which 49 have nine holes in the circle. At Jebel Al Fraiha Professor Hawkins counted 24 game boards and 62 rosettes.

If we accept that the parallel rows of cup-marks at these sites and others are, in fact, variations of the *mancala* game, then a number of problems occur. Foremost is the sheer number of boards. Why would anyone go to the trouble of carving out a new board each time he wanted to play? The game can be played just as easily on the sand, in instantly-created scoops, as on a solid surface. Then there is the apparently random number of holes, ranging from as few as two rows of three holes to two rows of 14, and even three and four rows of holes. I know from my own observations when I lived in Nigeria, where the game was widely popular, that although the numbers of holes and counters varied from region to region, within each region it was invariably consistent. The Yorubas of Nigeria always played with a 6x2 board and 48 counters, just as in Kuwait the board consisted of 7x2 holes and 70 counters were used. It seems inconceivable that the game players of Al Jassasiya played such a wide number of variations.

At Al Jassasiya and Al Fraiha some of the so-called game boards are carved on the sloping surfaces of the rock, where the cups could not possibly have retained any seeds, shells or pebbles used as counters. Some are so close to each other that there would not have been room for players to gather round them at the same time. And in some of the parallel rows of holes, particularly those with three and four rows, the individual holes are too small to hold any counters larger than a grain of rice.

So if the rows of cup-marks are not games, what are they? It has been suggested that the cup formations were used for the sorting and storage of pearls. But it seems highly unlikely that such small, precious, easily lost objects would have been exposed to a rough, windswept rock surface. Although in Qatar the cup-marks always occur in areas associated with pearl fishing, in other parts of the world similar carvings are to be found which can have no connection with pearls.

Another suggestion is that they were used in some way for divination. Some anthropologists believe that games involving counters were not conscious inventions but should be regarded as survivals from magical divination rituals. Yet another theory is that the series of rows of holes were systems for computing time and tides. Of the 333 sets of holes in rows, 193 consist of two rows of seven. When doubled the sum of the holes is 28, the approximate number of days in the lunar month. Twenty-eight is also, in ancient Arabian astronomy, the number of the moon's 'mansions': the groups of stars through which it passes as it progresses east.

Some of the bas-relief ship designs which are such a prominent feature at Jebel Al Jassasiya are simple representations of sailing vessels, but others incorporate lines and cup marks superimposed upon the outline of the ship. One, of a many-oared boat, with a rope and anchor at one end and trailing what may be a fishing net at the other, has been compared with the constellation of Orion, and the suggestion is that the cup marks represent stars. Another appears to resemble the constellations of Canis Venitici and Ursa Major. Undoubtedly, the people who made the petroglyphs on Qatar's limestone hills were familiar with the patterns of the night sky, and may have tried to influence the powers of the heavens above with their carvings below. To begin to comprehend the purpose of the cup-marks it may be helpful to compare them to other similar

carvings worldwide. Prof. Hawkins notes the similarity of the sites in Qatar to those of southern Scotland, where petroglyphs always occur on low horizontal rock outcrops with an open view of the sea. In both places many of the carvings have connecting lines running downhill. Many rosettes in Scotland closely resemble those in Qatar, except that they always have a circumferential ring. As in Qatar, they are associated with large 'basins' cut deep into the rock.

No date has yet been suggested for the Qatar cup-marks. Comparable carvings in Scotland are believed to date as far back as 3000 BC, but that does not mean that the Jebel Al Jassasiyah petroglyphs are as ancient. Some are more weathered than others, as the sand carried by the wind gradually scours the surface smooth. The unequal degree of erosion does not necessarily indicate the relative age of the carvings but the exposure of that particular site to the prevailing wind.

Large circular pits cut into the *jebel* at Al Jassasiya and Al Fraiha have been compared with fire-pits found throughout the Gulf region. In Iran they are associated with the fire-cults of pre-Islamic times. At both sites foot marks are carved into the rock, sometimes a simple narrow oval or pair of oval shapes but, in one example at Jebel Al Jassasiya, complete with toes. The making of foot and hand marks on rock and the painting of hand prints in caves is of extreme antiquity. Experts have dated hand prints discovered a few years ago in a cave near Cassis in southern France to 25,000 BC.

Top: A random pattern of cups linked by channels.
Right: Rosette of cup marks

More research still needs to be done on the rock carvings of Qatar. Meanwhile anyone who visits these lonely, windswept rocks is free to speculate as to the meaning and age of these enigmatic carvings.

BOAT CARVINGS OF AL JASSASIYA

AT AL JASSASIYA ON THE EASTERN COAST, NORTH OF THE OLD PEARLING PORT OF AL Huwaila, a long line of scattered limestone outcrops stand near a lonely shore, surrounded by barren desert. Many people who explore the landscape of Qatar at weekends are intrigued by the range of carvings on these low, wind-etched rocks, known as '*jebel*' in Arabic. Al Jassasiya was not always so isolated a site as it is today as indicated by the range of potsherds and other objects that were found near the rocks with the remains of a stone-built settlement to the south-east. These included a blue-glazed bowl fragment of the 13th-14th C. AD, water jars of the 14th -16th centuries AD and a Persian coin dated c.1700 AD.

Al Jassasiya is one of about a dozen major rock-carvings sites in Qatar, all but one being coastal. There are also numerous examples of petroglyphs on isolated rocks along the coast, but Al Jassasiya and Jebel Fuwairit, a little to the north, are the only sites with carvings of boats. On Jazirat Al Huwar off the NW coast of Qatar there are two *jebel* outcrops with petroglyphs of simple canoe-shaped boats, some of them over two metres in length, but these differ in style from the carvings on the Qatar mainland.

Unlike rock paintings, carvings are often

very difficult to date and no definite dates have been found for the oldest of the carvings in Qatar, although some similar designs in Oman have been tentatively dated to the 3rd millennium BC. As in Oman, where outlines of Land Rovers are depicted next to designs that are obviously more ancient, the carvings at Al Jassasiya have been added to at different periods up to and including the last century. They range from a series of configurations of cup marks, some with a surrounding ring, to two very different styles of petroglyphs depicting boats. It is possible that the earliest may belong to the Neolithic period, others could be a mere couple of hundred years old.

One type of ship carvings is made in bas relief, where the boats are shown in plan. The others are depicted in linear profile and the lines appear to have been 'pricked' onto the

Top: A group of oared boats in bas relief
Bottom: Bas relief boat with oars, trailing a metal anchor

soft rock surface with a metal tool.

The carvings were first photographed in 1962 by a Danish archaeological expedition led by P.V. Glob and the British archaeologist Geoffrey Bibby. A more thorough investigation of the site was carried out in 1974 by the Danish pre-historian Holger Kapel, whose son Hans meticulously planned and drew all the petroglyphs. They recorded a total of 124 of the bas-relief designs. Many of the boats are fish-shaped with sharply pointed sterns, with cross-seats, thwarts and the stepping for the mast clearly depicted. Some boats trail large anchors, either the metal European anchor (*bawara*) or the ancient Arabian form (*sinn*): a round or triangular stone attached to a rope, with a hole in the centre through which a beam of wood was fixed. These stone and wood anchors were in use well into the 20th century. In his guide to the pearl-oyster beds, published in Bahrain in 1920, the famous pearling captain Rashid bin Fadil Al-bin-Ali recommends them for certain anchorages, including Halul Island.

The design of boats and ships in use in the Arabian Gulf barely changed over many centuries until the coming of the oil era. The *boum* in which the merchant adventurer Sindbad the Sailor made his voyages over 1000 years ago, in the Abbasid period, did not differ greatly in overall design from the dhows which can be seen today in the harbours of Al Ruwais, Al Khor, Al Doha and Al Wakra. The ancient method of steering a boat was with a steering oar and some of the boats in the carvings show these at the stern; others have details that could be interpreted as a rudder. Some have a roughly carved appendage, which could represent a fishing net. Many have oars, depicted as straight lines at right angles to the hull. There are mostly six, eight or ten pairs of oars to each boat, although some have a seemingly random arrangement, with more oars on one side than the other. Some authorities believe that these petroglyphs represent boats on the pearl banks, where oars were used to manoeuvre about the banks and were left unshipped as support for the divers. It has also been suggested that they might be oared fishing boats for inshore use. The nearest thing to such a vessel today is probably the *badan*, a high-stemmed sardine boat still in occasional use in Oman and on the east coast of the UAE. This is a very ancient type of vessel with a rudder attached to the stern and operated with ropes. It is a rowing boat and two to four pairs of oars are used, but it does not carry a sail, so the ships of the bas-relief carvings, although similar in shape, cannot have been *badans*.

Badan on the beach

The big two-pronged metal anchor was first introduced into this area by the Portuguese in the 16th century, but smaller four-pronged grapnels are known to have been in use some 200 years earlier. So all that can be said is that the boats with metal anchors cannot be older then 700 years, at the most. And even that is not certain, because on one of the ships the rope and anchor appears to have been added at a later date, judging by the different patination of the carving.

On the group of rocks nearest to the coast, on the far side of the road that runs to the east of the main *jebel*, are a number of detailed line-cut drawings, in which grooves have been pricked out using a pointed metal tool and a hammer. There are 17 line drawings. They are interesting because of the number of recognisable types of sailing vessels. The artists were careful to include such details as would enable a ship, when seen at a distance as a silhouette, to be identified. One, a *battil*, has the characteristic fiddle-head pro-

Above: Linear depiction of a 'battil'.
Below: Linear depiction of a 'baqqarah'

jection at the bow and a high stern (*fashin*). In addition seven round-bladed oars are shown along one side and the ship carries both a triangular and a lateen sail, which may have been used in combination for certain wind conditions. The *battil* was a large, fast vessel, extensively employed in the pearling fleets but also useful as a warship. When a *battil* was on the pearling banks, the oars were used to manoeuvre it around. Photographs of the Qatar pearling fleet taken in 1929 show banks of oars with diamond-shaped blades. Another illustration may be of a *baqqarah*. A characteristic of the *baqqarah* is its projecting stern frame which enclosed the rudder stock. The stern post had a raised part at the back and is decorated. Both *battils* and *baqqarahs* were of stitched construction, in a tradition that pre-dates the influence of European shipping on Arab boat design that began in the early 16th century. On this vessel, as in some of the others, the lantern holder at the back of the ship

channels to a collecting jar, were uncovered in the 1980s excavations. Two more were discovered in 2002.

An unusual find in the first season was of a quantity of very large pearl oyster shells piled up in the corner of what had been an open courtyard. These were from a species, *Pteria macroptera*, which was mainly gathered for mother-of-pearl. The mother-of-pearl trade was controlled by Germany until the first World War.

Among miscellaneous small finds in the first season were several bronze coins, fragments of inlaid glass-paste bracelets from India and an attractive ring made of agate, probably of Yemeni origin.

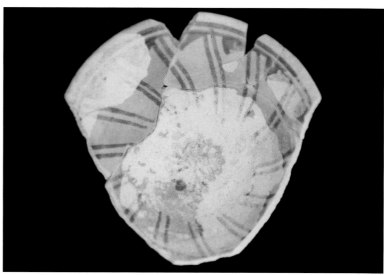

Manganese purple ware bowl, manufactured in southern Iran, 18th-19th century AD

Excavations the following year doubled the area uncovered in 2002 to 1600 square metres. A street became visible, running between the house walls. More date-presses came to light, and a

Left: Date press.   Right: Pearl oyster and mother of pearl shells

number of small finds gave glimpses of the lives of the people of this remote town. One was a small, green-glazed toy horse, minus its head and legs, similar to those already found in Iraq, the UAE and Bahrain. A tiny clay jar was crammed full of brightly-coloured beads made of semi-precious stones, glass and metal. Clearly the treasured possession of some girl or woman, its loss must have been mourned. A ten-centimetre-long shaped object crudely modeled out of bitumen proved to be something of a mystery. Munir Taha suggests that it might have been used for holding ink. The barrel of a small cannon, one of the very few weapons ever found at Al Zubara, may have come from a ship.

In 2004 excavations continued, when a further 700 metres square was uncovered. Ibrahim Kuwaitli, an archaeologist from Lebanon, joined Munir Taha at Al Zubara. The Geographical Informations Systems (GIS) in Doha installed datum points and benchmarks at the site, to facilitate the stratigraphic recordings made by the archaeologists.

A doorway in the recent excavations

In 2005 the archaeologists concentrated on the settlement at Fraiha, north of Al Zubara, with its small fort and scattering of houses. It appears to have been a 'satellite' of Al Zubara, probably established in the early 19th century when space within the walls of the larger town became scarce as the population expanded.

Al Zubara is a huge site, and there is much, as yet uncovered, which will provide material for archaeologists to study for generations to come. Some of the finds from the excavations of the 1980s can be seen on display in the nearby Zubara Fort, which was built in 1937 and was in use for many years as a police post until it was restored and designated as a temporary museum. There are plans for a large new state-of-the-art museum to be built adjacent to the fort in 2006, which will house not only archaeological finds from Al Zubara but from other sites in the north of Qatar.

HISTORY WAS MADE AT RAS ABROUQ

THE PENINSULA OF RAS ABROUQ, WHICH LIES NORTH OF DUKHAN ON THE WEST COAST of Qatar, is one of the most beautiful areas of the country. The entrance to it is dramatic: after driving across the featureless gravel plain which occupies the centre of the country, you leave the Doha-Dukhan road and take a newly-surfaced road north. The modern road goes only as far as the village of Bir Zekrit, and soon you enter into a different landscape, suddenly coming upon low, gleaming white cliffs of Miocene limestone, sculpted over aeons of time into strange contours.

Besides numerous plateaux, their sides hollowed by the wind and topped by a harder layer of sand and gravel known to geologists as the Hofuf formation, there are many free-standing mushroom-shaped pillars. Here and there the limestone is pierced with arches, worn by relentless wind-blown sand over the millenia. Further into the peninsula a large, natural oasis lies in a shallow depression, sheltered on one side by a limestone plateau. It is always green, even after months without rain, and when it does rain a carpet of fresh green grass covers the ground within days. Bitter gourd vines trail their tennis-ball-sized fruits over the sand, which in the spring months is starred with small yellow flowers. Thorny bushes and trees used to surround an ancient well next to a group of tall date palms, but the well has now been filled in and a shallow drinking pool has been provided for a small herd of sand gazelle which has been released at the oasis.

Numerous remains left by the ancient inhabitants of Qatar have been found throughout the Abrouq peninsula. Between about 5,000 and 3,500 BC a semi-nomadic population survived here by hunting, fishing and gathering shell-fish, wild grains and fruits, as well as herding sheep and cattle. Today their flint tools litter the ground, and dark, ashy patches on the plateau mark the remains of their cooking fires. Visiting sailors from Mesopotamia brought fine painted pottery known as 'Ubaid ware, fragments of which survive on a few coastal sites in Qatar, including Ras Abrouq, alongside the more primitive undecorated locally-made pots.

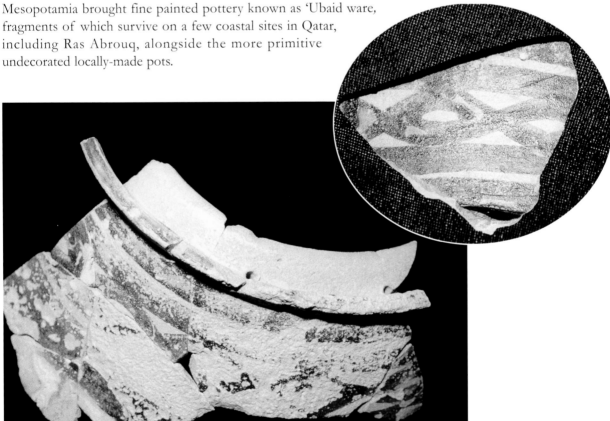

Left: Limestone mesa at Ras Abrouq.   *Above: Fragments of fine painted 'Ubaid pottery, imported from Mesopotamia*

Much later came the tent-dwelling pastoralists, the ancestors of the bedouin, moving through the area with their flocks of animals in search of water and pasture. No permanent housing was ever erected on the Abrouq peninsula with the exception of a small, fish-processing complex on the coast, dating to the early centuries AD. A square fort surrounded by a small settlement, built around two hundred years ago, was recently excavated by the French Archaeological Mission, directed by Dr Alexandrine Guerin. Not until the discovery of oil in October 1939 did the little village of Bir Zekrit, which stands at the entrance to Ras Abrouq, appear. The Gulf War resulted in the construction of some temporary military installations, while a coast-guard station was erected some years ago near the northern end of the little peninsula.

Then suddenly, everything changed. Just five years ago, hordes of picturesquely-dressed warriors mounted on Arab steeds charged across the landscape, their swords glittering in the sunlight.

A village came under sudden attack, and before long the palm-thatched roofs of the huts were ablaze. Sleepy Abrouq had certainly never seen so much activity in the eight millennia since human beings first entered the peninsula of Qatar.

A flashback in time? Ghosts from the past?

Not at all – Qatar Television was making a film!

Arab horse at film set in Ras Abrouq

The film, which was eventually broadcast as a long-running series, was entitled 'Eial al Deeb: The Sons of the Wolf'. It was by far the most ambitious project ever undertaken by QTV, with a budget more than twice as high as for any other previously-made films. Actors, actresses, cameramen and technicians were drawn not only from Qatar but also from Kuwait, Jordan and Syria. The expert horsemen were from Bahrain as well as Qatar, and several hundred soldiers were brought in to take part in battle scenes.

The long-running plot for this series was written by Ahmed Al Misnad, an established poet but a writer relatively new to television, who first approached the Director and Assistant Director of QTV, Ali Al-Qahtani and Talal Al-Attiyah, with his ideas and suggestions. Not closely based on historical fact, the story was set in Qatar some four to five hundred years ago. Much of the plot centred on the inter-relationships of the families within a little town, soap-opera style, with some breathtaking action scenes to liven up the story.

Hayat Al-Fahad, the well-known Kuwaiti actress, was one of those who played star parts in the film.

Film set at Ras Abrouq

Three film sets, designed by Jordanian Jamil Awad, were constructed: a group of circular thatched stone huts in a ravine encircled by a horseshoe of steep limestone cliffs, a tented encampment on the coast, and a superb 'mini-town' on the northern side of the Abrouq oasis. It is a conglomerate of easily recognisable features of traditional Gulf architecture: houses, minarets, wind-towers, *majlises* and enclosed courtyards jostle together in a fashion which might look a little odd in real life but is ideal as a film-set. The effect of this rich architectural collection, painted a pleasing honey-colour, in an arid landscape that has never before seen any construction at all, is surreal. The set was designed to last ten years, as QTV intends to make further films in the Abrouq area.

Meanwhile the set makes a pleasant focus for weekend visitors to Ras Abrouq. The tented village has gone, and the thatched huts were set alight during the filming of an attack, so all that remains are the curious round stone-walled structures around the ravine. One of them is perched high on a giant mushroom of limestone, up which a stairway had to be constructed. The traditional mini-town still stands and is kept under repair. The caretaker is always willing to allow visitors through the gate to take a look around.

Given the extremely delicate and fragile nature of the unique landscape of Ras Abrouq, there were, inevitably, concerns as to the long-term impact all this construction and activity would have on the environment. QTV personnel were keenly aware of the problems of possible damage and sought advice from senior officials from the Supreme Council for the Environment and Natural Reserves. Once filming was finished, the landscape was restored to its original state. Removing the thick, black carbon deposits from the limestone cliffs behind the fired village – the fires were made of car tyres soaked in diesel – was a major exercise. But all was left as clean as before filming began. There was even a bonus that resulted from the filming - the cleaning up of the oasis. This beautiful area was, sadly, often littered with rubbish left by careless campers and picnickers. Before filming, every last piece of trash was carefully collected from the landscape. Even car tyre marks had to be carefully swept out with a palm leaf brush before filming could begin. It would never do for a set of tracks, a cigarette butt or a soft drink can to appear in scenes that were supposed to be taking place five hundred years ago! Now, the oasis is surrounded by a light fence to keep out vehicles, and the only tracks are the delicate hoof prints of the *rheem* gazelle which wander to and from their drinking pool. They have recently been joined by a flock of ostriches. It is a heartening example of how simple, inexpensive repairs to a damaged landscape have greatly improved it as an amenity for all who visit Ras Abrouq — one that, hopefully, will be followed in other parts of Qatar.

Remains of film set stone huts at Ras Abrouq

Sailing dhow at sea

FOR THOUSANDS OF YEARS MEN TOILED IN DANGEROUS AND EXHAUSTING CONDITIONS in the waters of the Arabian Gulf, seeking ornaments for the robes of rulers and for the adornment of their women. Through their pain and misery incredible shining beauty, the lustre of natural pearls, came to light.

Pearls are found in two species of shellfish: *Pinctada radiata* and *Pinctada margaritifera*. They are formed by a grain of grit or a small parasitic worm acting as an irritant to the soft body of the oyster, which surrounds it with smooth concentric layers of nacre (calcium carbonate). These harden to form either free-moving spherical pearls or blister pearls which are cemented to the inside of the shell. Overlapping platelets of aragonite on the surface give pearls their characteristic lustre. They come in many colours, ranging from creamy white to golden yellow or rosy pink, through to deep grey and gun-metal blue, called black in the trade.

Oyster beds (*hayr*) are located in greater numbers on the Arabian side of the Gulf than on the Iranian side, probably due to the shallower depths on the western side, combined with sediments more suited to oyster growth.

The simple process whereby pearls are formed was not understood until recently and legends attempted to explain the seemingly miraculous appearance of pearls in oysters. They were said to be the teardrops of angels, or drops of rain which the oysters rose to the surface of the sea and opened their shells to receive.

The history of pearling in the Arabian Gulf goes back some 7000 years, to the period of the New Stone Age, when man first occupied the eastern coast of the Arabian peninsula. The oldest pearls yet identified are found at sites dating to the 6th/5th millennium BC, which were created by herding, fishing, hunting and gathering communities, generally referred to under the term 'Arabian Neolithic'. A pierced pearl from this period has been found in Kuwait, and other pearls are associated with burials in the United Arab Emirates, at a coastal site in Umm al-Quwain and an inland site in Sharjah.

As well as pearls, mother-of-pearl artefacts were also found at some of these sites. Undoubtedly, these resulted from deliberate pearl fishing, rather than accidental acquisition during food-gathering activities. The discovery of huge middens of oyster shells at a site in Eastern Saudi Arabia, together with microlithic drills used to pierce the shells and pearls, indicate an established industry, which may well have been the basis for trading with other communities.

There is a reference to 'fish-eyes' being imported into the Mesopotamian city of Ur in the early 2nd millennium BC. This unlovely name may be a reference to pearls: when a fish is cooked its eye is circular, white and opaque. However, some authorities think the reference may have been to polished, banded stones. Later in the millennium a scribe recorded on clay tablets the legend of the semi-mythical hero king Gilgamesh and his search for immortality. Following directions from Utu-nipishtim, the Babylonian counterpart of Noah, Gilgamesh attached stones to his feet and dived into the sea to find the 'flower of immortality.' This technique is strongly associated with ancient pearl diving.

Historians consider that the magical 'flower' was probably a pearl, which had associations with the concept of eternal life. The quest was centred in Dilmun, the Bronze Age trading empire that extended from its focal point in Bahrain to Qatar and up the eastern coast as far as Kuwait.

The first unequivocal reference to pearling does not occur until the 1st century AD, after which references to pearling and pearls in the Gulf become more frequent. By this time pearling was undoubtedly an established industry in the Gulf, supplying the Roman market and later the ruling elite of the Byzantine, Persian and Early Islamic periods. The Roman writer Pliny identified Tylos (Bahrain) as a specific locality associated with pearling. Pre-Islamic Arabic poets refer to pearl-diving and the dangers faced by the divers. In the 7th century, the beauty of pearls is referred to in the Holy Qur'an, where they are associated with Paradise.

Very early on, Bahrain became established as a leading pearling centre. The traveller Ibn Battuta, writing in the

14th century AD, said that boats with divers and merchants from Bahrain fished the banks in April and May. In the following century there is a reference to 1000 pearling ships from Bahrain. Another important centre was Julfar, north of the modern town of Ras al-Khaimah in the Emirates.

Both these places had established populations, with good water supplies and a high agricultural input. Julfar was nearly 300 km from the pearl banks (*hayr*) in the middle of the lower Gulf and over 400 km from the dense pearl banks off the coast of Qatar. There is no reference to Qatar as a pearling centre at this time and it would seem that centres for the trade were not necessarily those closest to the pearl banks. Instead, the industry was dominated by coastal areas, which had large enough populations and resources to equip sizeable pearling fleets.

The north coast of Qatar has the advantage of being located in proximity to the pearl banks. The Iraqi historian al-Masudi, writing in the 10th century AD, records that its waters were renowned for being rich in pearls. However, the population of Qatar at this time was not large enough to supply a major industry and significant pearling centres did not emerge on the peninsula until the 18th century AD.

The earliest centre associated with the pearling industry in Qatar was Al Huwaila on the north-eastern coast, which appears as Huali on the Niebuhr map of 1765 of the Arabian Gulf. Now a ruined site, which remains largely unexcavated, it was clearly a town of considerable importance from the 17th to the 19th centuries AD, judging by the extent of the ruined buildings and the variety of surface pottery. Another centre may have been at Ruwaidha in the far north-western coast, where a large fort dominates two areas of settlement. But from the mid-18th century onwards both these centres were eclipsed by the great pearling and trading port of Al Zubara on the north-western coast, which rapidly increased in size and importance after the al-Khalifah clan settled there in 1766. The town, which frequently came under attack, was surrounded by walls and guarded by Al Murair fort, constructed in 1768, and linked to the sea by a 2-kilometre-long ship canal the following year.

Besides the pearl oysters, another species, *Pteria macroptera*, was gathered for mother-of-pearl. During the ongoing excavations at Al Zubara, a pile of *Pteria macroptera* shells the size of dinner plates was uncovered, stashed in the corner of a courtyard where presumably they were awaiting export. Until World War I, Germany was the principal importer of mother-of-pearl from the Arabian Gulf.

Contemporary pearling centres founded in the 18th century were Kuwait City (1710) and Abu Dhabi (1761).

Jalbut pearl diving boat

Unlike Al Zubara, no previous centres had existed there locally.

Al Zubara, Kuwait City and Abu Dhabi are all located in areas where an inadequate water supply and little potential for growing food crops had limited previous settlement and expansion. This indicates that, unlike the much earlier settlement at Julfar in the northern UAE, fresh water and an agricultural hinterland were no longer essential for a pearling centre to develop. All the new centres had to import water and food to supply their growing populations.

By 1810 a British naval captain, John Wainwright, reported of the Arabian coast that 'Along its whole extent a valuable Pearl Fishery is carried on by the Arabs,' and many of the older pearling centres continued to flourish, headed by Bahrain. Other centres were at Dubai, Sharjah, Ajman and Umm al-Quwain. From the 18th century onwards, the families which controlled the pearl trade became established as local rulers. They were the Al-Khalifah of Bahrain, the al-Thani of Qatar, the al-Nahyan of Abu Dhabi and

Jalbut used in a documentary about pearl diving

the Al-Makhtoum of Dubai, who retain power to the present day.

In 1965 a British traveller, William G Palgrave, spent some days in Qatar. Seeing the numerous forts and towers scattered around the landscape, he observed that although the land outwardly seemed barren and poor, 'Katar has wealth in plenty, and there are robbers against whom that wealth must be guarded.' He visited Al Bidda (now the heart of modern Doha) as the guest of Shaikh Mohammed bin Thani, the founder of the ruling dynasty, who remarked to him, 'We are all, from the highest to the lowest, slaves of one master, Pearl.' All thought, all conversation, all employment turned on that one subject, commented Palgrave, and he describes the long lines of black boats drawn up upon the shore and the careworn appearance of the men inhabiting Al Bidda, who spend 'the one half of the year in search of pearls, the other half in fishery or trade.'

The following year Col. Lewis Pelly in his brief study of the pearling industry, explained that, 'The beds along the Arabian coast are held to be the property of the Arabs in common…an Arab of Kuwait may dive along the Bahrain or Ras-al-Khaimah coast and vice-versa. But no person other than the coastal Arabs is considered to have any right of diving.' He estimated that there were between 4,000 and 5,000 boats engaged in pearling along the Arabian coast, each boat containing from 10 to 32 men.

Diving occurred in the months when the warm water allowed repeated immersion. The diving season was divided into three. First came a 40-day 'cold dive' period beginning in the middle of April, called *ghaus al-barid* in some regions but known in Qatar as *al-khanjiyah*, followed by *ghaus al-khabir* (local name: *al-oad*), a long, gruelling stint from the end of May until the second week of September, and finally *al-raddah*, 'the return', a three-week period at the end of September and the beginning of October. Between these events there were breaks to allow the pearl-fishers to return to their home ports to re-provision and rest.

During bad weather the ships would sometimes make for the nearest shelter. The waterless Halul Island, situated 90-km off the coast of Qatar and adjacent to some of the best pearling banks, was often used as a haven by the pearl-fishers.

Pearls were also gathered in the winter, in a practice called *mujannah*, which involved wading and gathering

Pearl divers about to descend

oysters from the shallow coastal waters.

During the long periods when almost all the able-bodied men in Qatar were away at sea, their wives assumed the responsibilities of the head of the household, in charge of family finances and the care of children, the sick and the elderly. When they returned from the pearl banks the pearl-fishers handed over their earnings to their wives, if any remained after paying off their debts. It is evident that women at this time held an important role within the coastal communities.

Some pearl fishermen would spend as much as six unbroken months at sea, having taken out a loan from the boat owners to buy provisions for their families. An initial loan was usually paid in Indian rupees, the common currency at the time, and was known as *teskam*.

Each ship carried a captain (*nukhada*), usually a man with a lifetime's experience of fishing for pearls who could locate the best pearl beds without the aid of maps, relying on the observation of stars, currents and the state of the surface of the sea. The depth at which an oyster bed lay was measured by means of a *bild*: a large piece of lead at the end of a rope which was thrown into the water. The mud or sand which stuck to the lead also yielded information about the state of the sea-bed.

The pearl divers (*ghasah*) might be either free men or slaves. Their pullers, who hauled them up from the sea-bed, were called *siyuh*. There were also servants known as *tabbah* and sometimes apprentices, *walaid*. Each crew had a leader, the *macdami*. Boys as young as nine or ten (*radif*) often came along on the trips, to learn the secrets of pearl-fishing from their elders. Their job was to catch fish, help with the cooking, and make the coffee. One old diver recalled that he learned to swim at this age when his father tied a rope to him and threw him off the side of the ship!

The *nukhada* would announce the date of departure to the assembled men, after which those who wished to dive would step forward. They were then given an advance payment. On the day of departure (*al daasha*) the whole community turned out with songs and dances to bid their men farewell, and the *nukhada* would sometimes hand out small gifts of money to the divers' families, which was thought to bring good luck.

Music, including singing and dancing and the playing of percussion instruments such as the drum (*tabr*) played an important part on board, as a moral-booster and a distraction from the harsh and often dangerous working conditions. The lead singer was known as the

Pearl divers celebrating

nakham. A visitor to the pearling dhows wrote that, 'the singing, clapping and beating of rhythms never stops from dawn until sleeping time.' Before deciding which pearling boat they would join for a season, divers would make enquiries about the *nakham*; a lead singer with a good reputation guaranteed an enthusiastic crew. In good weather, the average diver made between ten and fifty dives per day, depending on his stamina. But exceptional divers were reputed to make as many as ninety dives. The depth of the dives averaged from 12-15 metres, but could be even greater. Some boats anchored on one pearl bank and stayed there the whole season; others moved from bank to bank.

The divers prepared themselves each early morning by fixing pincers of turtle-shell (*futam*) to their noses, plugging their ears with wax, and donning leather finger stalls (*khabat*) for protection from sharp shells and venomous fish. Cotton suits provided protection against jellyfish stings, and some divers believed that they helped guard against shark attack. Attacks were always more likely to happen towards the end of the season, when sharks had overcome their natural fear of humans and had become accustomed to food scraps being thrown overboard.

When ready, the diver placed his foot in the loop of a rope to which were attached lead or stone weights, and was dropped to the sea bed. There he collected the oysters into a bag (*dayeen*) hung around his neck or attached to his waist. When he could no longer hold his breath he gave the rope a tug to signal to his waiting puller to haul him up.

The usual method of retrieving the pearls was to leave the shellfish piled on the deck overnight to weaken and die, before prising them open with a sharp knife (*meflaka*). If a man found a pearl he lodged it between his toes. When the task ended the captain would retrieve the pearls. The shells, which often had tiny developing oysters attached to them, were then thrown back into the sea as 'nourishment' for the oyster beds.

Pearl divers opening the shells

This was the practice in the Arabian Gulf, but in other parts of Asia the oysters were taken to shore before opening. Excavations in 1981 and 2000 on a small island off the coast of Qatar revealed large shallow pits littered with fragments of oyster shell, dating to the 14th century AD. These may be evidence for an earlier alternative method of retrieving pearls. Two large pierced stones which may have been divers' weights were also retrieved at the site.

Divers and crew lived on a simple diet of dates, fish and rice, with dried limes to ward off scurvy. Working divers generally ate very little, to preserve their lean and wiry physique. Before the season began, some divers visited traditional healers, who would bleed them (*hejama*) using a glass cone. Divers often suffered from respiratory and ear problems and a popular form of treatment was cauterization with a hot iron (*al kaye*). In the evening after a day's dive the crews of different ships visited each other to exchange news and drink coffee. Ships belonging to feuding tribes would peacefully anchor side by side, as there was an agreement not to quarrel during the season. Buyers (*tawwash*) used to visit the fleet and go from boat to boat, bargaining for the catch. The name comes from that of the small rowing boat, also called a *tawwash*, which the buyers employed to ply between the pearl fleet and the shore. Another smaller boat called a *huri*, or a dug-out canoe known as a *ket*, was also used.

However, sometimes the pearls were returned to land before being sold. In 1866 Col. Lewis Pelly, the British Political Resident in the Gulf, made a study of the pearling industry and recorded that pearls of yellowish hue were exported to Bombay (now Mumbai) whereas the Baghdad market preferred pure white pearls, including seed pearls.

Before bargaining began the pearls, which were kept in a red cloth bag, were graded for size by being passed

Pearl divers examining the crop

through a series of circular copper or brass sieves with holes of various dimensions. The largest were known as *ras*, then came *batn*, in the third sieve *zayl* and finally *ruweiba*. The seed pearls which passed through the smallest sieve were known as *alsahtat*. Pearls were then further classified according to their quality, shape and colour. Those not perfectly spherical were called *barouque*. An expert could sometimes tell if a misshapen pearl contained a perfect one, and could peel off outer layers to reveal its beauty.

At the end of the season (*gaffal*) the money from the sale of the pearls was divided between the *nukhada* and the crew according to a prearranged ratio. The *nukhada* himself usually borrowed money from a businessman (*musaqqam*) at the beginning of the season to pay for provisions on board and give loans to the divers. The divers in their turn were often in debt to the *nukhada*, who charged them high interest on the loans. After a poor season it often happened that a captain could not pay off his own debts, and so had to sell the entire harvest of pearls to the *musaqqam* at 20% below market value. A diver who did not earn enough to pay off his debts had to continue working, sometimes for years. Debts were passed on to a man's sons when he died until, in the 20th century, some states passed laws to end the practice. The system of debt-slavery was endemic throughout the Gulf region, but was said to be less common in Qatar because many of the divers returned to a semi-nomadic existence at the end of the season, so that it was difficult to trace them.

All kinds of boats were used for pearling: the most common were the big *baghlah* and *battil*, but *boum, sanbuq* and smaller vessels were also employed. The generic term in use in Qatar for a pearling boat with oars and sails was *ghawwas*. The oldest boat surviving in Qatar is a *jalbut,* which was still in use as a pearling boat in the 1940s and is preserved at the National Museum. Some were built in the boatyards (*wushar*) of Doha and Al Wakra, others were ordered from the UAE. While on the banks the pearling fleets had to be guarded against piracy, and large, well-armed ships patrolled the fleet to give protection.

A century ago the principal pearl merchant families, besides the al-Thani, were the al-Sulaithi, the al-Khulaifi, the al-Noaimi of Zubara, the al-Mohannadi, the al-Kuwari, and the al-Majid of al-Wakra. The businessman Hussein Alfardan, whose father was a pearl merchant, is today internationally regarded as a leading authority on natural pearls. Until 1990 the house of Al-Haj Mohammed al-Majid, with an upstairs room overlooking the sea, still stood in Al Wakra: here the returning divers entered directly from the shore, to collect their salaries and repay any money they owed. Other merchants would gather to inspect and bargain for the season's harvest. By the end of the 19th century, the demand for pearls was global. The British Empire was an insatiable market for pearls and the markets of Europe and the USA also fuelled the boom. During the first two decades of the 20th century New York became the second biggest market for Gulf pearls after Bombay. In 1907 JG Lorimer in his *Gazetteer of the Persian Gulf* recorded that over 800 pearling ships sailed from 11 coastal towns in Qatar, the largest number (350) from Doha, with the majority of the adult male population engaged in pearling. But less than three decades later a death-blow crippled the industry, when the cultured pearl was developed in Japan. Experts can easily differentiate between a cultured and a natural pearl, but the average customer cannot and few were willing to pay the higher price for wild pearls, particularly when financial depression hit Europe in the 1930s. The Second World War meant that less money was available in the West for luxury goods and the trade suffered a further setback in 1948 when the Indian sub-continent gained independence from British rule. The spending power of the royal princes, who had long been among the industry's highest-spending clients, was curtailed.

'Jalbut' on the beach

Said al Bidad (left), a famous pearl diver, took part in the making of a pearl diving documentary in the 1960s

The combination of these factors was a major setback for the economy of the entire Gulf region. Two decades of severe hardship, during which many families emigrated from Qatar, were to follow, before the fortuitous discovery of oil changed the country's future. Many of the finest pearl banks now lie directly beneath the oil rigs.

A few boats still continued to fish for pearls until the late 1940s. A retired diver, Jassim bin Qroun Ibrahim al-Dosari, in an interview published in 1984, recalled, 'It was a very difficult period. Of the dozens of craft which used to go out in search of pearls all but a few lay idle in the harbour, and the boat I had been working on was broken up and used for firewood.' But a few years later, divers who had been earning 60 rupees for six months work were earning 25 rupees a month working in the growing oil industry. The days of bitter toil and hardship were over.

In conversation with an old pearl diver, a former British ambassador to Qatar once referred, rather naively, to the 'good old days'. Fixing the diplomat with a look of withering disdain the old man responded, 'For you, young man, half an hour then would be like a lifetime of hell.'

TRADITIONAL BOATS

THE PEOPLE OF QATAR HAVE BEEN SEA-FARERS FOR COUNTLESS CENTURIES.
Pearling, fishing and trading by sea were, before the advent of the oil era, vital to the existence of all the peoples whose lands bordered the Arabian Gulf. Along with their neighbours Qataris were accomplished boat builders, creating their wooden craft from imported timber.

A 'shasha', made from bundles of palm leaf spines

There were many different types of vessel, known collectively as dhows. Unlike European ships and boats, which are classified according to their sail rig, Arabian boats are distinguished by the shape of their hull.

The most common fishing craft of the northern Gulf were the *sanbuq, shu'i, jalbut* and *badan*. *Sanbuq* (pl. *sanabiq*) and *shu'i* (pl. *shawai*) are still in use today, and the *shu'i*, distinguished by its simple and elegant lines, is now the universal fishing dhow of the Arabian Gulf and Oman.

For inshore fishing and for travelling short distances along the coast from one village to another, *huri* (pl. *hawari*) and the *shasha* (pl. *shoosh*) were used until a few years ago. The former were dug-out canoe-shaped boats, while the latter were of a very ancient design, made from bundles of palm-leaf spines lashed together with rope made from beaten date palm stalks. They had cross-pieces made from Zizyphus or Acacia wood. These little craft were cheap and easy to manufacture and a fisherman usually had at least two, as they were not waterproofed and when the palm stems in one became waterlogged he would return it to the beach to dry out. Although fragile, their flexibility allowed them to ride heavy surf with ease. A *shasha* could carry two to four men and usually had two wooden oars, one located in the middle and one at the back.

The *shasha* is no longer manufactured in Qatar, but in Fujairah, UAE, there is still a builder of these simple craft. He says that he obtains 90% of the material for building them from the date palm and the wood for the cross pieces from trees growing in the mountains. However, nylon rope has replaced the traditional date palm stalk rope, and styrofoam blocks provide buoyancy instead of the section of date palm stem that was formerly used. Building a *shasha* only takes the master and his assistants five or six hours, provided all the materials are prepared beforehand.

Sanbuq, shu'i and *jalbut* (pl. *jalabit*) also served as trading vessels and cargo carriers, but for many years they were the Gulf pearling vessels and turned the area into one of vibrant commercial activity. A solitary example of a *jalbut*, a rather larger vessel than the others, can be seen at the lagoon of the National Museum and is easily recognisable because of its prominent upright stern. This particular boat was still in use as a pearling vessel until the 1950's.

The *sanbuq* has a high, square stern rather like the shape of a shield, which is embellished with flower and petal carvings. Some have blue and white decorations. They have a short keel, which old Qatari boat builders said was suitable for use in the shallow waters where the oyster beds were. It also made the boat more manoeuvrable with oars. Some types of *sanbuq* were double-ended and Bahrainis were traditionally famous for manufacturing these.

Shu'i, referred to by Gulf seamen as the sister of the *sanbuq*, are almost identical, the difference being the shape of the stemhead: the *shu'i* has a straight stem (the main upright timber at the bow of the ship) ending in a double curve while the *sanbuq*'s stem is cut off in a single concave curve. The tip of the *shu'i*'s stemhead is

usually painted blue. The stern has projecting strakes, which nowadays are often used to hold a platform on which fish traps can be carried.

Until the 1950s the *baggara* (pl. *bagagir*) was used for pearl-diving as well as for fishing and transporting goods. It was from 30 to 60 feet long and carried a cargo of between 10 and 30 tons. Another vessel much in use in days gone by was the *shahuf* (pl. *shawahif*), a fishing craft with a pointed stemhead and a long upright sternpost. A carving of a *shahuf* at the petroglyph site at Jebel Al Jassasiya shows the main features of this craft but without its rudder and mast. Today the *shahuf* is used for fishing with both lines and nets, but formerly it was also sometimes in use as a pearl-diving vessel.

A 'shahuf'

Another large vessel was the *baghlah*, a stately craft which measured up to 135 feet in length, with its stem curved and topped with a distinctive rounded figure-head. The largest and most ornate of all the dhows, it was rigged with two or three masts and had a low bow.

A light superstructure attached to the stern served as living quarters for the captain and his family and some elite passengers. It is believed that the *baghlah* came into use in the beginning of the 17th century after Arab sailors visited the shipbuilding yards of the English East India Company in Bombay.

The *baghlah* (pl. *baghlah*) was the traditional ocean-going vessel of the Gulf until supplanted towards the middle of the twentieth century by the *boum* (pl. *abwam*) which can still be seen frequently in the local harbours. Its richly carved transom stern was decorated with elaborate foliar scrolls and arabesques and pierced with five windows, a design influenced by that of the Portuguese ships that came to the Gulf in the 16th century.

Again, an example can be seen among the Jebel Al Jassasiya petroglyphs. The world's largest wooden sailing vessel is a *baghlah* built in Kuwait in 1998-9 as a floating hotel, the magnificent 'Al Hashemi II'. It has a length of over 269 feet and weighs 600 tons.

In Qatar, the largest locally-built wooden dhow currently is a 90 feet long *battil*, (pl. *batatil*) constructed by the master builder Yousef Al Majid in the 1990s. This elegant vessel can often be seen resting at its moorings near the Doha Corniche.

Decorated stern of the 'Hashemi II', the largest wooden sailing vessel in the world

In former days *batatil* were operated as pirate ships, coastal trading vessels and occasionally as pearling vessels. They were renowned for their speed. This made them popular long ago among slave traders who often had to defend themselves against aggressors or escape patrol boats endeavouring to put a stop to the trade.

A double-ended craft, the *battil* had a long, overhanging fiddle-headed bow, a high sternpost and double, forward-leaning masts. From the keel the after part rose up to form a thin stern-board, towering over the poop. A linear carving of a *battil* at Jebel Al Jassasiya shows clear evidence of this type of dhow, with seven round-bladed oars on one side and the characteristic bow and stern with the rudder in place. The drawing shows a triangular and a lateen sail, which were probably used in combination for different wind directions.

Because of their enormous size, *baghlah* were very expensive to build and craftsmen sufficiently skilled to construct vessels of this size were becoming hard to find. Therefore they gradually were replaced by *boum* and several examples of these can be seen at the jetties along the Corniche in Doha and at Al Wakra, Al Khor and Al Ruwais.

On board a 'battil', built by Yousef Al Majid

One of the finest ships in the maritime history of the Gulf, the *boum* (pl. *abwam*) is distinguished by its sharp, straight-pointed stemhead which is usually painted black and white. Though mainly used for trading, *boum* were also used for pearl diving. In the days of sail they had two masts; the main mast was raked forward and the mizzen mast was vertical.

Although the *boum* was, in general, smaller than the *baghlah* it replaced, it was cost effective as it was lighter, with better cargo space. Its pointed stern made it a much faster ocean-going vessel.

Before World War II, some ocean-going *abwam* weighed as much as 400 tons and carried six sails, with a crew of 40 men. But the commonest type of *boum* ranged in weight from 60 to 200 tons, with a length varying from 36 to 120 feet. They were frequently used to carry mangrove wood from East Africa and teak from India. Some transported rocks or stone, cement and even trucks to Gulf ports. They were also equipped with tanks to transport water and in the pre-oil era many *abwam* were in use carrying water from Bahrain, which had a plentiful supply owing to its many natural springs, to thirsty Qatar.

The *boum* is believed by some authorities to have derived its hull shape from the pre-Portuguese period, as there are marked similarities to medieval illustrations of ships. A feature of the medieval ships is also the high, straight bow angled at 45 degrees, which is such an eye-catching feature of the modern dhow.

The shift from sail to engine power took place in the 1950s, although the traditional shapes of the dhows were retained. The awe-inspiring sight of a fleet of ships under full sail, setting out for the pearling

A 'boum'

banks, is now, alas, a thing of the past. Almost no one living in Qatar today with the exception of a few elderly *nakhudas* (boat captains) and their crewmen will have been fortunate enough to witness it.

The change from wooden to fibreglass hulls is more recent, but some boat owners still prefer the traditional wooden hulls. Both have their advantages and drawbacks. Fibreglass dhows are made up, layer by layer, inside a wooden mould. They lack the beauty and grace of wooden dhows, but are economical to construct, since several dhows can be made successively in the same mould. Fibreglass boats ride higher in the water, since there is no timber to be saturated and require less maintenance. But if anything goes wrong and the dhow is damaged it is far more complicated to repair than a wooden vessel. So it seems that the days of the wooden dhow are not yet over and, hopefully, they will continue to be built in Qatar for years to come.

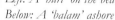

Above: Gargour fishtraps on a fishing boat
Left: A 'huri' on the beach
Below: A 'balam' ashore

UNTIL THE MID-TWENTIETH CENTURY, BOAT-BUILDING YARDS FLOURISHED UP AND down the Gulf. Although many of these have now closed, the building of dhows is still a living tradition. It is one of the most evocative images of the past, but is now having to survive against the onslaught of modern technology. Within a couple of generations, boats that were once widely in use have now become objects to be displayed in 'heritage' museums, along with the tools used in their manufacture.

Of all the craftsmen once associated with dhow building, only the master-builder survives. The craftsmen with whom he would once have discussed the building of a new dhow and its various requirements: the blacksmith, ropemaker, flax spinner, weaver and sailmaker, are long gone, and only the dhow-builder is left to hold together the art of building a dhow.

Although it still survives in Qatar, the centre of dhow-building is concentrated in the UAE and buyers from Saudi Arabia, Bahrain, Kuwait and Qatar now travel to the small Emirate of Ajman where the most extensive yards are to be found. The majority of the dhows ordered are *shu'i*, used for fishing.

A few dhows are built in each of the other Emirates, with the largest boats being constructed in Dubai. The owners of the yards are nationals, but their workforce comes entirely from India, where there is also a very long tradition of building wooden boats.

Until the advent of the Portuguese in 1488, ships were constructed from hewn planks, fastened together with coconut-fibre cord held in place by wooden pegs. Later, iron-nailed framing was used in the hulls. The ancient Gulf craft were always double-ended, with a pointed stern, and would have carried a steering oar mounted close to the sternpost. Gradually square-sterned boats came into use, with high, elaborately carved sterns influenced by the design of Portuguese and Dutch vessels of the 15th and 16th centuries.

Probably the last 'sewn' boat to be constructed in this region was in Oman in the early 1980s, when the adventurer Tim Severin re-created the kind of vessel Sindbad the sailor might have used and sailed it to China. The boat, a *boum* named Sohar, belongs to the government of Oman and can be seen on display on the roundabout near the Albustan Hotel in Muscat.

The methods and tools of the boat-builders have changed remarkably little over the centuries. In the dhow yards today it is still possible to observe boat-building skills that may well date back thousands of years, still practised in much the same way. Construction work is carried out without the use of plans or drawings. All measurements for the variations are memorized by the builder. When discussing the building of a dhow with his customer, the master-builder (*jallaf*) will sketch the ship in the sand with his finger, or on a plank with some chalk, detailing some parts. As a master-craftsman, he would not be happy if the customer tried to pin him down to precise measurements. The whole business is based upon mutual trust: the builder and customer discuss the measurements of the dhow, a price and an estimated completion date are agreed, and then the transaction is sealed with a handshake. It is then up to the builder to provide the best boat he can for the price.

While the master-builder is a local, sometimes assisted by his sons who join him after school to learn the family trade, his highly experienced carpenters come from India or sometimes Pakistan. The master-builder's employees are the *zarrab*, the carpenter who fastens the planks with nails, the *imzawri* who

Detail of badan showing stitching at the stern post

Boat builder working with simple tools

carries the timber from the yard to the ship, and the *imleid*, the boy who clears up the yard and whose important task it is to keep the kettle boiling on a scrap-wood fire to provide tea and coffee for the workers.

The building season for dhows traditionally begins in October, when day temperatures began to fall, and ends at the beginning of June. A relatively small *shu'i*, used for fishing, can take about three months to build, with bigger dhows taking anything up to nine months. Almost all Gulf dhows follow the shell construction. The keel is laid first, with the ribs of the ship which run from the keel to the side rail being inserted after the planks on the outside have been fitted in. This is contrary to the method used in the West, in which the planks are fitted to a rib-skeleton.

In the past, the laying of the keel was an anxious time for the dhow builders, and a new keel was usually guarded or protected by a fence. There was a belief that if a woman who had had difficulty in becoming pregnant could jump across a newly laid keel she would conceive a male child, but that the *djinns* which watched over the dhow would inevitably take a life for a life. So the carpenters worked as quickly as possible to lay enough planks to make a barrier too high for any woman to jump over! In northern Europe there was a somewhat similar superstitious belief that if a witch could cross the keel she could attack the boat at sea. Therefore a piece of elder wood, long held to be efficacious against witch-craft, was sometimes inserted into the keel.

In a traditional boat yard, the first impression the visitor receives is of the pleasant smell of newly cut timber, mostly teak, together with the more powerful odour of shark oil. Untidy piles of adzed branches of trees, known as '*jangali*' (jungle wood) lie about here and there. In the height of summer the branches are sometimes piled into the sea, to keep them from splitting in the intense heat.

Above: Shell construction of 'dhow'
Right: Sailing dhow leaving the harbour

Teak from India was always the preferred wood for the boat builders. Its use in Bahrain for the construction of seaworthy and durable vessels was noted by the Greeks more than 2000 years ago. Nowadays, teak is becoming scarce and prohibitively expensive. Teak is used for the hull and mangrove poles and jungle wood for the ribs. Owing to the cost of these materials, many dhows today are being built from fibreglass in a wooden mould, but some owners still prefer to have a traditionally made wooden boat.

The tools employed are basic. In Kuwait as late as the mid-1980s logs were still being cut into planks using a pit saw, this would take days of concentrated skill in the exhausting heat. Despite the introduction of the electric drill in many yards, some old shipwrights still prefer to use a bow drill to bore holes for the iron nails. They claim that an electric drill can burn the wood and that the bow drill is cleaner and safer. The carpenter uses an adze, a thin arching blade set at right angles to the handle, to fair off the planks with gentle strokes. The adze, saw, chisel and auger, little changed from their original design, have been in use in eastern boatyards for thousands of years, as ancient drawings and writings testify. Once the adzeing and planing of the planks is finished, they are carefully slotted into grooves along the keel,

Using a bow drill

and into the stem and stern posts which have already been bolted to the keel. The first planks are the most difficult to fit, as they must have a pronounced twist to give the shape of the boat, and much hammering and tapping is required to get them just right. They are then nailed into place and small blocks of wood are fixed temporarily on the outside to help the planks keep their shape.

Only as the ship grows are the ribs, made of crooked lengths of wood, fitted inside it. Eventually all the planks will be nailed down to the ribs, the nail holes making neat lines running up the sides of the ship. The holes are made wider at the outside so that the large heads of the nails may be countersunk. If a bow drill is being used then the men have to chisel out the holes for the nail heads with an auger. Once the nail is in place the hole is stopped with mastic.

Nails to fasten the planks are still manufactured locally by ironsmiths in Bahrain and Kuwait, along with the hinges for doors and the gudgeons and pintles which hold the rudders. Some carpenters prefer galvanized factory-made nails from India, although they are more expensive, because they are harder. The nails come in many different lengths, each for a different purpose; the longest are the ones used in the keel. Yousef Al Majid, the Qatari master shipwright, who built the beautiful *battil* which can often be seen at its moorings at the Doha Corniche, said that he

Putting a nail in the planks

Above: Toilet box hung on the stern of a boat
Left: Ornamental carving

preferred iron nails to the galvanized factory-made type because they were firmer and more durable. In his boatyard the nails were carefully wrapped in oiled fibre before they were inserted, to help ward off the rust which eats into the wood and spoils the appearance of the boat.

Once the planks are all in place a *piece of* soft cotton string impregnated with fish or coconut oil is driven into the joints and then the whole boat is oiled with fish oil, or sometimes coated with hot pitch, to make it waterproof. Below the waterline a coating made from boiling oil and animal fat mixed with burned lime is applied, to deter barnacle growth and give protection against the wood-boring worm, *teredo*. Shark oil is applied to the topsides and the interior. The oil intensifies the rich colour of the mahogany.

Then the finishing touches are added: the deck, the cabin and nowadays, the engine and propeller. Dhows with engines are known as *lanchaat*. Finally the toilet, a round box with a hole in the floor, is hung over the stern of the boat.

The larger dhows may have carved decorations. The carved rosette or 'eye' amulet design, elaborate on large boats and usually painted red, blue and white, has degenerated to a simple eye painted on the prows of some *shu'i*.

Finally, the dhow is ready for launching. This is always an occasion for celebration and feasting. In the old days the whole village would turn out for the launching of a boat, and in the yards in Ajman, UAE, everyone lends a hand to help get the vessel into the water. A path to the sea is cleared, rows of logs are greased to act as rollers and truckloads of old tyres are placed on the left side of the dhow. Props are knocked away until it subsides onto the tyres, and, rather inelegantly, it is pulled and pushed by a bulldozer until it slides into the sea on its side.

Once it has reached deeper water the dhow rights itself and glides proudly out over the blue-green water, accompanied by singing, dancing, the beating of drums and hand clapping from the excited watchers on shore. In the days of sail, the last job to be done before the dhow could start its maiden voyage was the fitting of the masts, rigging and sails, and this was always done while the dhow was afloat.

A NOTABLE FEATURE OF TRADITIONAL ARCHITECTURE IN QATAR IS THE NUMBER AND variety of its forts, especially of those along the northern coastline. In days gone by, when attacks on settled populations by marauding desert tribesmen were a constant threat, it was essential for people to have strongholds to which they could retreat in times of emergency. Sometimes these were no more than isolated, windowless round towers, with an entrance half way up the wall, which could be reached by a ladder or a rope that could be pulled inside.

In addition to attacks by robbers intent on plunder, there were many disputes between neighbouring tribes over territory and water, so communities had to be constantly alert to the possibility of danger. Apart from its importance as a place of security, a fort also served as the residence of the chief of the tribe and was a powerful and impressive symbol of authority. It could be seen from far away across the flat desert terrain, surrounded by the humbler mud-plastered stone dwellings, huts and tents of his followers. It was also a landmark recognizable from far out at sea.

Above: Barj Barazan before reconstruction
Left: Reconstructed Barj Barazan showing buttressing

The typical desert fort was rectangular and built of rough blocks of limestone or flat slabs of beachrock (the Arabic name for this is *furoush*) to a height of two metres. Above this, solid walls of small mud bricks were built, and the whole structure was then given a thick, smooth coating of mud or gypsum plaster. Obviously, such a type of building required constant maintenance, particularly after the rainy season. After they were abandoned in the first half of the last century most quickly fell into ruin.

Each fort had a combination of round and rectangular or square corner towers, apparently entirely at the whim of the builder. On the north-west coast, for example, Al Thaghab has three round corner towers and one rectangular tower, whereas Al Rekayat, less than three kilometres away, has three rectangular and one round corner tower. Inside the forts villagers would need to store food and water in case they were besieged, and usually a well was dug in one corner. There would be a storeroom for dates and larger forts often had a *madbassa*, a room for processing dates. This had a ridged floor which was covered with palm leaf matting, on which dates were piled. Their weight caused the sweet sticky date juice to run down the channels into a collecting jar set into the ground in one corner.

Above: Beak-like projections at Al Wajba fort

Some forts, for example the one at Al Wajba west of Doha, had slit spaces in the wall under beak-like projections from which arrows or guns could be aimed downwards when the enemy got close enough. Wajba fort dates from the 19th century and is thought to be the oldest standing fort in the country, although the oldest forts of all, which have been dated to the 8th century AD, are among the ruins of the settlement of Murwab in the north-west of Qatar. Al Wajba was the headquarters of Sheikh Jassim bin Mohammed al-Thani on the famous occasion in 1893 when he and his men routed the Turkish occupying forces, who were forced to retreat to their own fort, the al Khoot, in what is now the centre of Doha. The latter is commonly known as Doha Fort and, until recently, was home to the ethnographical museum.

The corner towers at Wajba fort have simple external buttressing which is typical of some styles of fortified building; other examples of this can be seen on the two fortified houses built in 1910 by Sheikh Jassim's son Sheikh Mohammed.at Umm Slal Mohammed, about 20 km north of Doha city.

Visible from the main road leading to the north of Qatar are the recently restored towers known as the Barj Barazan. These were also constructed on the orders of Sheikh Mohammed bin Jassim, possibly as surveillance towers, although the number of rooms within the towers suggests that they were also used as a residence. 'Barazan' means a high place which can be seen from far away, and it is said that pearl divers could see the towers from their ships when they returned home.

Forts had narrow openings in the wall which widened out on the inside; here the defenders could stand and aim their arrows or firearms in all directions. Gates, always a weak spot in the defences, were made of thick wood studded with heavy nails, into which a small door was inserted, just big enough to allow one person, stooping, to enter at a time. Some forts had a recess just above the gate from which stones etc. could be hurled onto the heads of the attackers.

Although in some cases reduced to little more than low piles of crumbled mud and stones, with a surface scatter of potsherds, the string of forts around the coasts are instantly recognizable because of their shape. In 2005 two were under excavation: Zekreet fort in the south-west, where the French Archaeological Mission completed a third and final season of excavation, and Fraiha fort, a few kilometres north of Al Zubara, which has recently been excavated by archaeologists from the National Council for Culture, Arts and Heritage. There is a local belief that Zekreet fort was constructed on the orders of Rahmah bin Jabir, the famous chief of the Al-Jalahaimah who harried Gulf shipping for 40 years. If this is so it can be accurately dated to between 1809 and 1812.

Zekreet fort is unusual because, apart from a similar ruined fort at nearby Bir Hussein, also popularly attributed to Rahmah bin Jabir, there are no other forts on the southern coasts of Qatar. It appears to have had gypsum plaster on the lower levels of the walls and around the south-facing gateway, which was framed by solid pillars of palm-tree trunks. It has a scattered settlement of small houses around it, and in 2005 the archaeologists uncovered the remains of a substantial building between the fort and the shore, housing three date-presses.

Fraiha fort appears to date to the mid-19th century and has a small settlement around it which was probably a 'satellite' of the town of Al Zubara, a short distance away.

The town of Al Zubara, surrounded with substantial walls in the 18th century which were extended with a line of solid drum towers in the 19th century, had its own fort inside the settlement. This was built in 1768 to guard the town, which suffered repeated attacks from both land and sea. In 1769 a ship-canal was dug to link the fort to the sea. Not far away, on the eastern side of the road which runs beside the ruins of the old town, are the ruins of another much larger fort, M'rair, now almost completely destroyed.

Another Al Zubara Fort today forms a spectacular landmark on the coast a kilometer north of the old town and is comparatively new. It was constructed on the orders of the Ruler, Sheikh Abdullah bin Jassim al-Thani

Zubara fort

in 1938, as a response to the claims of Bahrain on Al Zubara and the construction by the Bahrainis of defensive fortifications on the nearby Huwar islands. This square, honey-coloured structure, with its crenellated parapets and sturdy corner towers and an old cannon standing beside the entrance, is one of the best-known of the peninsula's buildings, ever popular with tourists and photographers. Occupied by the police until about 15 years ago, it was then taken over and restored by the Department of Museums and Antiquities. It now houses some of the pottery, coins and other artefacts discovered by archaeologists at the old ruined town of Al Zubara, which can be seen from the upper storeys of the fort.

The archaeologist Geoffrey Bibby describes a visit to Zubara Fort in 1957. 'We pulled up at a more modern fort, a white-washed stone building with the flag of Qatar flying above it. It was a police post and we were greeted by the police detachment as a welcome break in the monotony of their lonely watch. Our escort had many friends among the little garrison and we were immediately given mugs of hot sweet tea, to last us while coffee was being brewed.'

When my family came to Qatar 20 years ago the Zubara police were still hospitably entertaining visitors with tea and biscuits. Our children were impressed when informed that dangerous prisoners were incarcerated in the upper rooms of the corner towers, reachable only by ladders, whereas lesser felons enjoyed the comparative freedom of the courtyard during daylight hours!

Above: Al Thaghab fort after reconstruction
Inset: Detail of ceiling at Al Thaghab fort
Below: Doorway at the reconstructed fort of Al Rekayat

Al Thaghab fort lies about 10km north of Zubara on the eastern side of the road. The fort was 19th-century, as can be determined from the pottery fragments and scraps of Indian glass bangles scattered around. However the remains of a scattering of houses which surround it may be of earlier date. Al Thaghab has recently been restored by the National Council for Culture, Arts and Heritage. Just north of Al Thaghab is the small fort of Al Rekayat, reconstructed by the Department of Museums and Antiquities in 1988. It is smaller than Zubara fort, but no less picturesque.

A few kilometers south of the town of Al Ruwais lies the huge ruined fort of Al Ruwaidha, next to a shore where, more recently, stands of mangrove trees have been planted. Al Ruwaida is an enormously impressive site because of its sheer scale, comparable to that of any Roman fort in Europe. The walls are now reduced to long mounds of crumbling mud brick and stones, but it is clear that a large population must once have flourished here, to build and maintain such a structure. This and the other forts provide ample evidence that the population of this north-western region must have been far greater in the 18th and 19th centuries than it is today.

Ruwaida Fort is older than the other forts, as is clear from the 18th century pottery sherds scattered on the surface. British archaeologists led by Beatrice de Cardi, visiting the site in 1973, found pottery sherds dating back as far as the 10th century AD, indicating that the site had been in occupation since then. Ruwaida is a site which would be worthy of excavation in the future.

All of these sites make interesting focal points for weekend explorations, and with a little imagination the visitor can picture life as it was in those far-off days, 'before the oil came.'

Courtyard of Al Rekayat fort

57

CAMPING WITH THE BEDOUIN

NOWADAYS, MOST PEOPLE IN QATAR, WHETHER LOCAL OR EXPATRIATE, REGARD CAMPING as a pleasant weekend pastime. It is hard to realise that within a short space of time, well within the memory of many citizens, setting up home in a tent was the normal way of life.

For thousands of years, the nomadic population of the country, known as *bedu* or *bedouin*, travelled the desert sands, always moving on in search of fresh pasture for their camels, sheep and goats. The term *'bedouin'* derives from the Arabic *badawi,* meaning 'without a settled home', and is in fact a double plural as *'bedu'* in Arabic is already a plural form, the singular being *'bedui'*. However, Westerners commonly speak of *'bedouin',* and then compound the error by adding an 's'!

There are pastoral nomads in many parts of the world: the Turkoman, Kirghiz and Mongols of Central Asia, the Pashtun of Afghanistan , the Lur of Iran and the Tuareg of NW Africa are among several that spring to mind.

Although their lifestyles and customs differ in many ways, all nomads share the same necessity to move according to the seasons and the availability of water and grazing. Their journeys recognised no national boundaries, but with the introduction of modern borders and such tiresome necessities as passports and visas, the nomadic way of life became difficult to maintain. Many countries actively discourage nomads from trying to cross borders.

In the Arabian Gulf, the fixing of national borders coincided with the oil wealth that changed the lifestyle of entire peoples and rendered the harsh life of the bedouin unsustainable, once people began to want the luxuries that go with a settled lifestyle. More and more men found employment in oil-related work. For a while their wives and children and the old people continued the lifestyle of tent dwellers, with the oilfield workers returning to their families at weekends. During the 1960s the practice gradually died away, as the government encouraged families to settle so that the children could attend school. Some tribes settled earlier than others, but in Qatar, within two decades of the first oil-derived cash which flowed into the country at the end of the 1950s, almost no families were following the old way of life. A lifestyle which had continued without a break for at least three thousand years had disappeared without a trace.

In 1959 a Danish ethnographer, Klaus Ferdinand, together with a noted documentary film-maker, Jette Bang, armed with notebooks, tape-recorders, cameras and film cameras, arrived at just the right moment to record the old way of life before it vanished. For three months, from January to the end of March, they travelled and camped with the bedouin. Both took thousands of photographs, both in colour and in black and white, and Jette Bang also made a short colour documentary.
Many years later, in 1991-93, Ferdinand put together the best of his and Bang's photographs into a

Opposite page: Al Naim tribe member with calf wearing a suckling-preventer of hedgehog skin. Above: Al-Murrah camp at Uglat Al-Manasir, South Qatar, 1959

Loading the camels at the Al-Murrah camp at Uglat al-Manasir, South Qatar, 1959

superb book, with the text based on material from their notebooks. He also drew on material and information collected by some of his Danish colleagues, the archaeologists and historians who were working in Qatar in the 1950s and 60s. The book was published in English by the Carlesburg Foundation in Denmark as part of their extensive Nomad Research Project.

While in Qatar, Ferdinand and Bang went first of all to the north near the old ruined city of Murwab, to spend some weeks with the hospitable Al Na'im people, and later shifted south to travel with the Al Murrah in the south. The two tribes had very different lifestyles; the Al Na'im were only semi-nomadic by this time, and kept chickens and pigeons, which would have been an inconvenience to people constantly on the move. They also used donkeys rather than camels as beasts of burden, as well as motorised transport.

An Al-Murrah woman feeds a child from a bowl, 1959

In the hottest part of summer, the Al Na'im lived in simple houses constructed of sea-rock or limestone blocks, or in palm-leaf huts known as *barasti*. The tents would be set up beside the permanent dwellings, so that when the temperature soared the families could retreat to the comparative coolness and shade of the houses.

During the cooler months of the year the Al Na'im set up two other camps. One was an autumn camp and the other was used during spring. All the camps were in the same area. The people explained to Ferdinand that in former years some of them used to migrate to Bahrain for the hottest months, transporting their camels by dhow. Water was always available in Bahrain, owing to the plentiful natural springs.

It was not long after the beginning of the oil era before modern artefacts turned up in bedouin encampments. Most useful of all were the inner tubes of large tyres, which could be used to transport water, looking rather like giant black sausages. Telephone wire for tying goods to pack animals proved stronger and lasted longer than the traditional hand-made ropes.

The Al Murrah people, whom the Danish researchers joined after spending some weeks with the Al Na'im, considered themselves to be one of the purest of the bedouin groups and were fiercely proud of their way of life. They were camel breeders and kept saluki dogs, which were often treated almost as members of the family, as well as falcons. During the autumn months they made short migrations, which gradually became longer once the winter rains arrived, their journeys taking them through wide regions of desert.

Pitching or dismantling the heavy striped woollen tents was strenuous

The saluki, favourite companion of the bedouin

work, undertaken by the women, while the men busied themselves with making coffee and caring for the falcons. Not surprisingly, for short stays the travellers sometimes simply erected a temporary shelter, made from one of the wall panels of the tent, or a tarpaulin.

Cooking was done in a shallow hole dug in the sand in front of the kitchen section of the tent. The pots and pans were kept in coiled, leather-covered lidded baskets. Other articles in daily use, including babies' cradles, were slung from the tent poles.

Besides the kitchen area the tents had separate sections for the men and their guests, and for women and children. There were one or two sections where everyday family life went on, but many daily activities took place in the area in front of the tent. A section of the main area of the tent was used as a store, and also by anyone wanting to take an undisturbed nap during the day. Additional woven partitions to give extra privacy could be quickly put in place. Very young animals were sometimes penned in a section of the tent at night for safety. Side cloths extending from each end of the tent, sometimes curving around in front to semi-enclose an area, gave some privacy and protection from blowing dust and sand. If the wind shifted direction these could be quickly moved.

When visitors arrived by vehicle, it was considered good manners for them to drive up to the back of the tent, to allow the women time to cover themselves with their *abayas* and withdraw to their own part of the tent if necessary.

Not only did the women set up and dismantle the tents, they also made them, weaving the long, dark brown and cream sections and the strengthening bands which were sewn to them, as well as sewing or pinning the sections together once the tent was pitched.

"In ordinary daily life everyone had a job to do, especially the women, who worked all the time," commented Ferdinand. The women spun wool or goat hair as they walked, and wove small articles such as udder-covers for the milk camels on simple hand looms held between the toes as they sat on the sand.

The milk camels and their foals were taken away from the camp around mid-morning by the herdsmen, in search of grazing, and returned to the camp just before sunset or sometimes later. Milking took place in the evening. Pack camels were simply hobbled and allowed to wander around in the vicinity of the camp

A member of the Al-Naim tribe with goat and kid, 1959

in search of their own grazing.

When preparing to move, everything had to be packed into bags which were slung onto the camels. Ferdinand and Bang were glad to have the opportunity of helping their friends by using their vehicle to assist with the moves, and also with fetching water when needed.

The grandchildren and great-grandchildren of the bedouin with whom Ferdinand and Bang spent such a pleasant stay less than half a century ago still enjoy camping during the cooler months, but nowadays a desert camp is likely to have a generator and electric lights, and even air-conditioning and a TV! The desert campers of the 21st century enjoy the pleasures of the simple outdoor life without any of its hardships.

Al-Murrah girls plait their hair and spin sheep's wool, 1959. Background: Citrullus colocynthis, the desert squash

THE CAMEL AND THE BEDOUIN

FOR THOUSANDS OF YEARS THE BEDOUIN OF ARABIA AND THEIR CAMELS LIVED IN A symbiotic relationship in which each was important to the existence of the other. The bedouin name for *Camelus dromedarius*, the one-hump dromedary, is *Ata Allah*, which means 'Gift of God'. Their camels provided the desert-roaming nomads with everything from milk and meat to wool for weaving and leather to be made into a whole range of useful articles. Small wonder that their owners regarded them as a gift from God, helping them to survive in a harsh world that gave them little else.

The story of the gradual development and domestication of this animal is a very ancient one. The earliest pre-historic relative of the camel lived in North America some 65,000,000 years ago and was the size of a hare. Later, from the Middle to Late Miocene era, it evolved into a tall creature called *Aepycamelus*, with long legs and an S-shaped neck. Like its modern descendants, this proto-camel moved both legs on one side of the body at the same time, a movement called pacing.

Around 5,000,000 years ago prehistoric camels migrated from North America to North East Asia via a land bridge which existed then. The ancestors of the humpless New World camels spread southwards to South America, where they evolved into guanacos and vicunas. From this wild stock the llamas and alpacas were domesticated. In North America the early camels disappeared about 10,000 years ago, probably hunted to extinction by the indigenous peoples.

The development of the Old World camel is harder to trace. It used to be thought that both the one-humped camel and the two-humped camel (*Camelus bactrianus*) derived from the same wild species (*Camelus ferus*). But recent research has shown that each of the two species has a separate ancestor. Over the last few years archaeological excavations in the UAE have provided new information about the wild ancestor of the domesticated dromedary. The earliest camel bones found were unquestionably those of wild animals, and there were signs that they may have been hunted and butchered. But later finds, of bones dating to around 1000 BC, correspond to the period when some researchers think that one-humped camels began to be domesticated in Arabia. Others consider that it may have been even earlier. One theory is that it could have been frankincense traders as far back as the 3rd millennium BC, who first trained camels to make the long and arduous journey from southern Arabia to the northern areas of the Middle East.

Others theorise that they were first domesticated as milking animals before they were employed as beasts of burden. Later, they became used as riding animals. There are accounts of ancient battles being fought by camel-riding Arab warriors, the Amorites, as long ago as the 9th century BC. The grave of a warrior dating to the Sassanid period, after 225 AD, was excavated some years ago at Al Mazrouah, north of Doha, and an intriguing feature was the presence of remains of camels around the grave. Early literature refers to the hamstringing of camels around the grave of a hero.

THE CAMEL AND THE BEDOUIN

Among non-desert dwellers, camels have the reputation of being bad-tempered and obstinate creatures which spit and kick. In fact, nothing could be further from the truth: camels are, on the whole, docile, patient and intelligent. The moaning and groaning noises they make when they are loaded up and trying to rise to their feet, which sound to human ears like grumbling, should be compared to the grunting noises and heavy breathing of a weight-lifter in action. Nevertheless, camels can bite and kick when angry, and a male camel in 'must' should always be approached with caution during the breeding season, when the bellowing animal inflates a red skin 'balloon' and projects it from its mouth.

The mutual affection of camel and bedouin owner is legendary, and the bedouin are said to have loved their camels on a par with their children. The famous explorer Wilfred Thesiger, who crossed the Empty Quarter in southern Arabia with his bedouin companions in the 1940s, described how, several times a night, a female camel would approach her sleeping owner to sniff gently at him as he lay beside the camp fire, carefully stepping over the bodies of his companions as she did so.

The long eyelashes of the camel protect the eyes from the sand, the nostrils can be closed and the mouth can browse on sharp thorns

The body of a camel is perfectly adapted for survival in the harsh extremes of the desert climate. Although it loses moisture through the skin, just as humans do, the camel has a unique and extraordinary method for conserving water loss. It can close its nostrils to conserve moisture and keep out sand and dust, and in addition experiments revealed that it is also able to extract moisture from expired air. The camel can minimize the quantity of water lost by the natural processes of urination and defecation.

Camel urine is intensely concentrated – four times that of humans. Camel droppings are dry, powdery balls containing almost no moisture. For that reason they have long been used by desert-dwelling peoples as fuel for fires.

Although camels can go for long periods without drinking, when given the chance they take on board vast quantities of water, far in excess of what their bodies have lost. In one experiment some camels were denied water for three weeks and then provided with an unlimited water supply. The camels drank at the rate of 60 litres per minute, and one animal managed to put away 186 litres! Normally such rapid ingestion of liquid would result in the swelling or even rupturing of red blood corpuscles, but the red corpuscles of camels are apparently able to withstand the strain.

The brains of mammals are heat sensitive and under extreme conditions the brain can heat up: this causes heat-stroke in humans, which can be fatal. But the camel has a unique inbuilt air-conditioning system, lacking in other mammals, enabling it to survive in the soaring temperatures of an Arabian summer. As the camel inhales, air flowing over its large nasal surfaces forms a layer of dried-out mucus. This mucus absorbs moisture when the animal exhales, which cools a network of small blood vessels around the jugular vein. When the cooled blood reaches the brain and eyes it lowers the temperature of the most sensitive cells by more than 4° C.

The Danish anthropologist Klaus Ferdinand and the photographer and documentary film-maker Jette Bang, when travelling with the Al Murrah in the south of Qatar in the spring of 1959, observed how their companions made use of practically everything from the camel, even its urine. The camel, Ferdinand observed, was the focal-point of their occupation and central to their way of life. When people from different families met, the subject of their conversations was often the welfare of their camels and the possibilities of grazing. A British anthropologist, Roger Webster, who studied the bedouin of Qatar for his doctoral thesis, described how, whenever the herdsmen worked with the camels they stroked them, talked to them or sang to them constantly. In *Arabian Sands*, published in 1959, the British explorer Wilfred Thesiger who journeyed into the vast and waterless Rub al Khali, or Empty Quarter of the deserts of Arabia, said of the Bait Kathir who were his travelling companions, 'They could tell at a glance from the depths of the footprints whether a camel was ridden or free, and whether it was in calf. By studying strange tracks they could tell the area from which the camel came. Camels from the Sands, for instance, have soft soles to their feet, marked with tattered strips of loose skin, whereas if they come from the gravel plains their feet are polished smooth. Bedu could tell the tribe to which a camel belonged, for the different tribes have different breeds of camel, all of which can be distinguished by their tracks.'

The camel was the bedouin beast of burden, riding animal and a source of rich, nourishing milk. Its urine was used for washing hair, to which it imparted a rich shine and it was said to help keep down lice. In addition, urine was used in tanning leather. It was the job of the little girls to follow the camels around with collecting bowls, and Ferdinand describes them 'leaping in like cockroaches' whenever a camel obliged!

Dried camel manure made excellent fuel, and it had another use, as a dry absorbent lining for babies' nappies. Jette Bang, who formed a very close and affectionate relationship with the bedouin women, describes how mothers of young infants had a supply of the light dry balls of manure on hand, which they crushed into powder. This was used to dry and clean the nappy area, before handfuls of the powder were used to line a clean cloth wrapped between the baby's legs.

Camel wool was spun and twined for a wide range of articles: cords of all thicknesses, socks to wear in summer for protection against the searing sands, bags, blankets and all kinds of equipment used on the camels themselves. Camel wool comes in all shades of natural colours, from cream through every shade of brown to almost black, and so was often used undyed. The wool used for the long striped tents, however, was dark brown goats' hair with bands of cream-coloured sheep's wool.

The skin was turned into leather, again used for a variety of useful articles, in particular for large transport bags. It also provided water-containers, but by the time Ferdinand and Bang travelled with the bedouin, these were being superceded by the inner tubes of tyres.

Although men, women and children all had their roles to play in relation to and in working with camels, ultimately they were the responsibility of the men. The owners and herdsmen had the true responsibility for breeding and daily care, and an important part of their work was milking their camels.

All lactating camels wore – and still wear – an udder-cover to prevent unchecked suckling by their foals. Ferdinand wrote that it was necessary that the foal was nearby or was even suckling during the milking. Milking normally took place from the left side, while the foal suckled from the right.

If the foal died its skin was stuffed and used as a dummy during milking. Sometimes another foal was put to the mother and her nose was blocked so that she could not tell by scent that it was not her foal. A good mare would give 2 to 3 litres of milk at a time. Camel milk could be drunk fresh, or put into tea, or made into a kind of yoghurt called *laban* which was kept in a skin bag.

Pack camels were only assembled for moving camp; the rest of the time they were hobbled and turned loose without supervision. The result was that when the decision was made to strike camp and move on, it often took a day or two to locate the pack-animals.

Female camels with foals were kept separate from the male pack-animals and generally cared for by herdsmen. Young girls also sometimes looked after the camels and little girls were often given the job of putting hobbles on the legs of the camels. When on the move, women and girls rode in a large, cushioned wooden litter called a *maghbat*. It had a curved framework which could be covered with cloth to provide shade from the sun and to conceal the passengers from passers-by.

Although camels are no longer essential to the way of life in Qatar, many families still like to keep herds of camels. Large numbers can be seen wandering in search of vegetation, particularly on the southern and western coastal regions, with their herdsmen never far way. Camel racing is a popular sport in most Gulf states including Qatar, and a pure-bred animal can fetch the same kind of astronomical price as an Arab race-horse. It seems that the day of the camel, at least in the Arabian Gulf, is far from over.

WHAT'S IN A NAME?

RECORDING THE PLACE-NAMES OF QATAR

THE PLACE NAMES OF A COUNTRY CAN YIELD A WEALTH OF INFORMATION, NOT ONLY about geographical features but about the people who gave the names, and what they considered important about a particular location. Maps of Qatar made by Europeans from the mid-eighteenth century onwards recorded, for the most part, only the coastal pearling and trading ports such as Al Zubara and Al Huwaila, and it was not until oil was discovered less than sixty years ago that there was a need for more detailed cartography. But until September 1995 only 700 place names had ever been recorded and many were wrongly transcribed, often because the cartographers were foreigners who in some cases were not even Arabic speakers. It was decided that this situation had to be rectified, and so the Qatar Geographical Names Survey was set up.

In 1996-7 a team of researchers from the Geographical Names Survey set to work to make a complete record of the place names of Qatar and in doing so came up with a wealth of fascinating sociological and cultural information. The researchers were recruited by the Centre for Geographical Information Systems (GIS), which was in the process of producing up-to-date and accurate maps of Qatar, using the very latest technology.

How do you go about organising such a huge information-collecting survey as this? Obvious sources of information about place names were the memories of elderly people, but getting in touch with the right people was initially not easy.

After some failures, the researchers hit upon the idea of approaching the seven different municipal authorities of Qatar for help. They prepared maps with the existing names and presented them to the local authorities. These proved extremely helpful in supplying the names of possible informants, and eventually a list of around sixty old people was compiled.

There was no time to be lost, because the researchers were afraid that some of the informants, who were in their eighties, might pass away before they had time to complete their survey. So during the summer of 1996, despite the heat, the teams roamed the length and breadth of the country daily from morning to night. There were nine people involved in the surveys, divided into three teams. Each team included a fluent speaker of English and Arabic. Other team members arranged the appointments and took charge of the Global Positioning System equipment which recorded the precise coordinates for each site.

Team members soon discovered that the best time to visit the villages and gather information was the early evening when, like old people everywhere, elderly men and their friends met together at the *majlis* to chat, drink coffee and set the world to rights.

Qurayn Balboul

Obtaining precise information about place names took much time and patience, because the old folk often argued fiercely and at length about the exact pronunciation and derivation of each name. The researchers followed the disputes with interest, often gaining extra information that way.

Getting to know the older generation of Qataris was a most rewarding and pleasant occupation for the researchers. They were overwhelmed by the kindness and hospitality shown to them by the local people, and by the enthusiasm shown for their work.

Old ladies were not directly interviewed by the male researchers, but sometimes when they were talking to an elderly man in his home his wife would listen and dispute with him about the correct names. In Al Khor one elderly lady who was known to be an authority on the area was sent a map and proved to be most helpful in identifying and naming new sites.

The usual method of checking the information, once a name had been decided on, was to ask the informant to accompany the team to the location, to be sure it was correct and to get the coordinates using GPS. This scrupulous attention to accuracy led to a dramatic incident in the searing heat of August 1996. One team

Al Khuwaimat

nearly came to grief, together with their informant who had a reputed age of around 100 years, when they got lost in the desert sands near Abu Samra on the border with Saudi Arabia. The vehicle became bogged down in soft sand and the radio failed to work. The water supply ran out and two members of the team set off to walk to Abu Samra to get help from the police. By the time they got there they were severely dehydrated. The police immediately launched a rescue operation and in the end the team members were none the worse for their adventure. They were, however, deeply impressed by the way in which the apparently frail old gentleman was little affected by the heat and thirst, whereas the researchers, whose average age was some 70 years less than his, were on the point of collapse. They had learnt their lesson, and on future trips into the remoter regions they never travelled without a second vehicle and plenty of water.

Within six months, working every day, the bulk of the survey had been completed. Along with the exact location of each site its particular features were recorded, along with the pronunciation of its name. The accurate recording of the place-names of Qatar yielded a wealth of information on the closeness with which a desert-dwelling people observe the slightest variation in the landscape. An area of sand-dunes south-west of Al Wukair is named Naqa Abu Dolou. 'Dolou' means ribs in English and the name refers to the rib-like ripples formed by the wind on the surface of the sand.

In the north-east of the country is a sandy area with two low mounds called Al Nehaidat, and the name derives from 'nahd', the Arabic word for a woman's breast.

Above: Ummahat al Maghati - the Place of the Covers
Right: Umm Al Jamajim - the Place of the Skulls

The name Al Zubara, in the north-west of the peninsula, rather surprisingly means a sand-mound. Sand is not an outstanding feature of the place today, especially when compared with other places in Qatar, but perhaps there was more in former times.

'Doha' derives from a word meaning 'roundness', a reference of course to the C-shaped bay around which the city is constructed. The name is found elsewhere on the country's coastline.

Other geographical features had been given fanciful names from their resemblance to everyday objects.

A cone-shaped hill, Qurayn Balboul, would be 'Spinning-top Hill' in English. And an obviously tent-shaped hill in the south-west naturally received the name Al Khuwaimat.

The deep cave which lies to the right of the Salwa Road opposite the Satellite Earth Station is named Dahl al Misfir. '*Dahl*' means a cavern, and '*Misfir*' means brightness, because of the bright light in the cave entrance when seen from within. Charmingly, the term is also used to describe the beauty of a woman who has just unveiled her face.

An area with strangely-shaped stones bears the rather sinister appellation of Umm Al Jamajim – the Place of the Skulls – and a craggy promontory with the profile of a cat's head is named Al Qita.

An interesting area in the centre of the peninsula has some unusually deep, natural holes in the rock: these were kept carefully covered by the bedouin with large, flat stones to conserve the precious rain water which collected in them. And so the place became known as Ummahat Al Maghati: the Place of the Covers. Three surrounding fertile areas (*rawdhats*) derive their names from this feature, which was once an important source of water.

Some places had been incorrectly named on maps by oil company geographers in the early years after World War II. One of these was Umm Said. It is now given its correct name of Messai'eed, which refers to a particular kind of soil found there.

Countless place names derive from trees, plants or shrubs. Umm al Tuwaim Al Gharib, a fertile area in south-west Qatar regularly visited by the nomadic bedouin in former times, is named after a perennial shrub, *Aerva javanica*, called 'Tuwaim' in Arabic. Its fluffy seed heads were used for stuffing pillows and saddle pads. That attractive coastal plant, *Limonium axillare*, which bears stiff bracts of purple flowers and is

'Qetaif' - Limonium axillare or Sea Lavender

Above: 'Tuwaim' - Aerva javanica Below: 'Markh' - Leptadenia pyrotechnica, inset: flower

known as Sea Lavender in English, is called 'Qetaif' in Arabic and so yields the name Qetaifan for an area on the coast north of Doha. A species of desert broom, *Leptadenia pyrotechnica*, with tough branches and small yellow flowers which dots the coastal areas is '*markh*' in Arabic and gives its name to Al Markhiya. Abu Samra itself is named after the *Samr* (*Acacia tortilis*) trees which grow there.

In a land where, until recently, land ownership by individuals was relatively uncommon, the concentration upon geographical or botanical features was inevitable, the names yielding important information to travellers. There are some place names derived from individuals associated with a particular area, but they are in a minority.

In a mere 18 months the number of place-names recorded in Qatar jumped from 700 to an astonishing 3,500: a tribute to the diligence and perseverance of the research team members. The teams estimated that they covered 11,000 km in their journeys.

That of course, was only the beginning of the story. Back in Doha the mass of material had to be studied, compared with existing information, discussed with experts and re-confirmed before being entered into the database.

Finally the names were stored in a National Archive which is freely available to the public. They joined the 400,000,000 names from all over the world which are stored in Geneva by the United Nations, in a database which is constantly being updated.

SAND DUNES AND THEIR FORMATION

THE LANDSCAPE OF QATAR IS NOT RENOWNED FOR ITS DRAMATIC VARIETY.
There are no lofty mountains, no craggy hills, no tumbling rivers and shimmering lakes. But Qatar boasts a geological phenomenon which, world-wide, is very rare: the singing dunes.

There are two major types of sand dune in Qatar, the great crescent dunes known as *barchan* in Arabic, and transverse or *seif* dunes, which are long and straight and usually lie parallel to the prevailing wind. They tend to form in desert areas where the wind blows mainly from one direction but where there are cross winds, whereas *barchan* dunes form in areas where the wind blows from one direction only.
Barchan dunes also occur on Mars, but this chapter will confine itself to the dunes on Earth, and those of Qatar in particular.

The area of *barchan*s known as the 'singing dunes', which lies between the Salwa Road and Messai'eed, has long been popular with both locals and expatriates for weekend picnics and fun, whether it is careering up and over the dunes in a 4WD vehicle, scrambling up their steep slopes to be rewarded by a spectacular view from the top, or sand-boarding down the sides.
World-wide, there are only 35 known sites where the barchans make the extraordinary 'singing' which so fascinates the visitor and we are privileged to have such a rare phenomenon here in Qatar. Not only do the dunes emit a most impressive humming and roaring as people slide down, but individual footsteps produce a strange squeaking sound. It is guaranteed to keep the kids happy for hours.
The singing of the dunes has been known and speculated about for many centuries. The bedouin, the traditional nomadic inhabitants of the deserts, attributed the noise to the voices of *djinn* – spirits which inhabit the desert landscapes, and which also manifest themselves in the eerie 'dust devils' which sometimes rise up and career hither and thither across the desert floor.
In the 13th century Marco Polo, who was also a subscriber to the *djinn* theory, said that the dunes 'sometimes fill the air with the sounds of all kind of musical instruments, and also of drums and the clash of arms.' A bit imaginative perhaps, but one gets the general idea.

The intrepid desert traveller Wilfred Thesiger describes the sound rather more accurately in *Arabian Sands*, his account of his journey into and across the Empty Quarter in the late 1940s: 'While we were leading our camels down a steep dune face, I was suddenly conscious of a low vibrant hum, which grew in volume until it sounded as though an aeroplane were flying low over our heads. The camels plunged about, tugging at their head ropes, and looking back at the slopes above us. The sound ceased as we reached the bottom. This was the singing of the sands.'

Left: barchan dune. Right: barchan dunes on a satellite photo

In recent times, scientists have come up with various theories to explain the phenomenon, and in 2004 Bruno Andreotti from the University of Paris set out in a determined attempt to solve the mystery once and for all. The French physicist took his equipment to the Atlantic Sahara in Morocco, which contains more than 10,000 *barchan*s. He and his team studied one of the large crescent dunes which are said to sing spontaneously all year long, sometimes two or three times in an afternoon, if it is windy enough. I have never come across dunes in Qatar which sing spontaneously, but evidently they occur in Morocco.

The wind forces the sand to accumulate at the top of the dune until the angle of the slope reaches a tipping point of about 35 degrees. The eventual avalanche of sand produces the singing noise. The sand has to be very dry for this to occur. The best days for the phenomenon are when there is no wind, so that the sun can dry out the dune face.

Not having the time or patience to sit around and wait for the dune to start doing its stuff naturally, Andreotti's team induced avalanches by sliding down the dunes.

By measuring vibrations in the sand and air, Andreotti was able to detect surface waves on the sand that emanated from the avalanche at a relatively slow speed of about 40 metres per second. The dune acts as a huge loudspeaker – with the waves on the surface producing the sound in the air.

Andreotti explained these sand waves as resulting from collisions that occur between grains at about 100 times per second. In a kind of feedback loop, the waves synchronize the collisions, so they are all on the same beat. This is why the low pitch – between 95 and 105 Hertz – has so often been compared to the noise of a low-flying propeller-driven aircraft. The maximum loudness of the singing is about 105 decibels.

So there you have it. The research is still not completed, because the sound seems in some way to be connected to the actual shape of the individual grains of sand. And there seems to be no satisfactory reason why some *barchan*s among the local 'singing dunes' will belt out a tune while their seemingly identical fellows remain obstinately silent.

It is fascinating to learn how barchans form. Often, the perfect crescent-shaped hills of fine sand seem to simply appear by themselves in the middle of a dry, windswept floor. The explanation seems to be that the breeze carries billions of grains of sand as it blows across the desert floor and if the wind drops, so do the sand grains.

Eventually there is a little pile, perhaps snagged against a small rock or bush. When there is more sand arriving on the wind than is being blown away, the dune starts to form. It develops its own stability as its lee side grows steeper and steeper, until there comes a point at which fresh dry sand simply rolls down it. Barchans most often form atop gravel plains or salt flats.

Formed into crescents by the relentless pressure of the wind, the barchans, which can reach 30 metres in height, move imperceptibly across the landscape, driven by the prevailing *shamal* wind from the north-west.

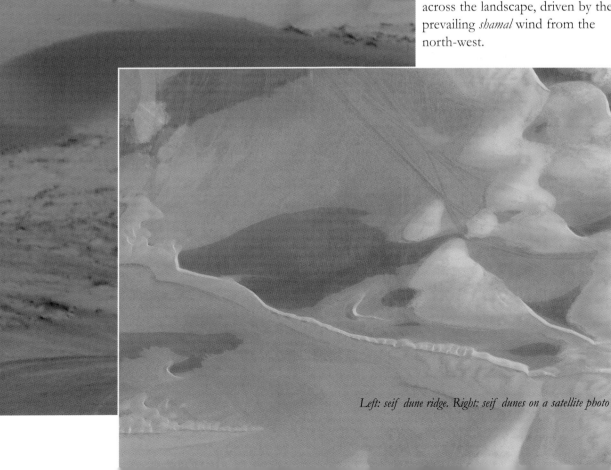

Left: seif dune ridge. Right: seif dunes on a satellite photo

SAND DUNES

A group of *barchans* can transform into a long, transverse *seif* dune if the wind changes. A cross wind causes the *barchans* to become elongated, each extending a 'limb' at one end. If the wind continues in the same direction the limbs will continue to grow and join together and the *barchans* will change their shape completely. This process can be observed among the great rolling dunes which march relentlessly south, across the land between Messai'eed and Khor al Adaid, the 'Inland Sea'. Once there, they continue into the water and if they continue at the same rate it may be that, one day, the whole of that shallow lagoon will be filled with sand. *Seif* dunes in other parts of the world have been known to form continuous ridges up to 160 kilometres long. Generally, they form sets of parallel ridges separated by areas of sand or gravel plains which create interdune 'corridors'. The long axes of these dunes extend in the resultant direction of sand movement. *Seif* dunes can be much higher than *barchans*, often reaching over 100 metres.

If engaging in the exhilarating sport of dune-bashing – roaring up and down the dunes that lie between Messai'eed and the Inland Sea — keep a sharp lookout for the changes in shape which can happen within a few days. Sudden precipices may form as the wind changes direction, and a dune which was quite safe to ascend and descend one month may develop a near vertical surface the next. Whether you are dune-bashing or enjoying the gentler pastime of exploring the singing dunes, either way the sands of Qatar are a great place to have fun. The best time to be on top of a dune is at sunset, when the red ball of the setting sun seems to hang above the desert, the golden sand is bathed in a luminous violet light and long, dark shadows form across the landscape, creating a delicate tracery where the wind has rippled the sand.

*T*HE TRUFFLE HUNTERS

AFTER THE WINTER RAINS, THE DESERTS OF QATAR BLOOM. WIDE SWATHES OF silvery-green tasselled grasses form on the gravel plains, and in the shallow depressions where the thorny scrub bushes grow the ground is starred with tiny yellow, pink and blue flowers. They attract myriads of feeding butterflies and other insects, while birds and darting dragonflies come to feed on the insects.

The desert blooms too with dozens of black or white-clad figures, all of whom walk slowly, their gaze fixed on the ground at their feet. Their faces wear the concentrated expressions of people who have dropped their car keys.

Whatever appearances may suggest, these searchers are not looking for lost possessions. No, they are treasure hunters, intent on finding a rare and expensive delicacy: desert truffles. Every year, if there is sufficient rain early in the winter season, truffles form just under the sandy or rocky desert surface, and searching for them is a time-honoured weekend family pastime.

Known as *fuga* in local Arabic, the desert truffles are botanically distant cousins of the truffles of Europe, which they do not resemble in taste or appearance. Yet they are locally as popular as the famous truffles of France and Italy are in Europe, where they fetch almost unbelievable prices at auction. In 1993 Perigord truffles, sometimes referred to as 'black pearls', sold in London at $1450 a kilo, and the same year Italian truffles reached a record high price of $2,200 a kilo.

The truffles of the Arabian desert have never commanded quite such dizzying prices, but they are considered a luxurious delicacy and many local families prefer the challenge and satisfaction of finding their own.

Inset left: Utetheisa pulchella, a day-flying moth. Inset right: Plain Tiger butterfly.

Possibly it is the secret and mysterious nature of truffles which has fascinated truffle addicts for countless centuries. Theophrastus, a pupil of Aristotle, referred to truffles in the fourth century BC as, 'one of the strangest plants, without root, stem, branch, bud, leaf or flower.' They grow out of sight, but always in the proximity of *Helianthemum* plants that are perennials.

Truffles appear to have been enjoyed by the rich and famous from the very earliest times: hieroglyphic texts on papyrus mention that desert fungi were served to the pharaohs of ancient Egypt. Three thousand years later, the tables of the Fatimid caliphs in Cairo were graced with truffles gathered in the nearby Muqattam hills. They have long been credited with possessing aphrodisiac properties.

The subterranean fungus is a delicacy

No one has ever succeeded in growing truffles under cultivation, despite continuing experiments. Traditionally the bedouin of Qatar, who were expert truffle hunters, believed that they were spawned by lightning and a clap of thunder, just as they believed that Arabia's other great treasure, pearls, were formed by oysters rising to the sea surface and receiving drops of rain. It is no coincidence that the precious winter rains should be credited with the creation of both these marvels. A local bedouin expert said that the number and size of the truffles are directly influenced by the number and strength of the crashes of thunder during a storm. As the growth of truffles depends on the amount of rainfall, there is a grain of truth in this belief.

Truffles are found in arid areas all around the Mediterranean, especially along the North African coast from Morocco to Egypt and further east across the great desert plain between Damascus in Syria and Basra in Iraq. In all these regions, people gather truffles for food. They go by different names in different places and many varieties are found in Arabia. In Qatar the two main varieties are *khalasi* or *jubei* and *huber*. The former are oval with a dark skin and a pinkish interior and have a robust, nut-like flavour. Some people prefer the second type, the creamy-coloured *huber*, with their more delicate flavour.

Helianthemum lippii, the host plant for the truffle

Zubaydi, another popular truffle, is also found here and more are imported from

Algeria, Morocco, Libya, Iran and Egypt, which sell for anything up to QR 200 per kilo. Truffles can usually be found for sale during the early months of the year at the back of the Salwa Road vegetable market and in a lane at the side of the nearby Omani market. Sometimes, Asian expatriates working in Qatar go out into the desert at weekends and offer the truffles they find for sale beside the main roads.

Usually no more than a few centimetres across, but sometimes as big as a man's closed fist, truffles are light in the hand, weighing anything from 30 to 300 grams.

The skin can range from a pale sandy brown to a deeper chocolate hue, and some have a reddish tinge. They are roughly spherical, but with a tendency to irregular lobes and bumps, and have a slightly spongey texture.

Experienced searchers for truffles know to look for truffles in slightly hollow areas that may dry out more slowly than level or hilly ground. They know, too, to look for certain plants that grow in symbiotic partnership with the desert truffle, especially varieties of a rock rose, the *Helianthemum* species. Fungal filaments of the truffle penetrate the roots of the other plant, sometimes reaching as far as 40 centimetres to do so. It is thought that in return the truffle produces a substance that inhibits competing plants.

In Qatar *Helianthemum kahiricum* and *H. lippii* are common and can be recognised, even by those without knowledge of botany, by their narrow oval greyish-green leaves and small, pale yellow flowers. Small, shrubby plants, they reach from 10 cm to 30 cm in height. They are known locally in Arabic as *ragroug*.

The best time of day to look for truffles is either in the very early morning or at sunset, when any slight rise in the sand casts a shadow that indicates a truffle might be hiding a few centimetres below.

I found my first truffles, many years ago, by shamelessly following a group of bedouin ladies hunting for truffles in the desert until they took pity on me and kindly showed me how to look for the slight rise and the faint cracks in the surface of the ground which are the clues to the presence of truffles growing beneath.

My first efforts were not a success; being unsure exactly what I was looking for I threw away the first two I found, mistaking them for pebbles! I know better now, but lack the patience of the truly successful truffle hunter.

Once found and brought to the surface, desert truffles have two enemies, sunlight and humidity, so need to be speedily taken home and prepared. They are not happy being kept in plastic bags and storage in the refrigerator does not prolong their life. Better to keep them in a shaded room with an air conditioner blowing cool air over them, if they cannot be prepared and eaten at once.

Traditionally, the bedouin roasted truffles in the ashes of their campfires or boiled them in camel's milk. Lacking either a campfire or a handy camel, many western expatriates prefer to boil them in cow's milk. Occasionally, gifts of truffles from generous Qatari friends come our way. We find that they are also excellent fried gently in butter for a few moments, with a sprinkling of rock salt and black pepper. Whatever method you use, truffles require the minimum of cooking, like mushrooms. You should also recognise that, no matter how carefully you clean them and slice them, their method of growth traps pockets of sand in the folds of the fruit body. So be prepared for a slight crunchiness!

Background: Cornulaca monacantha

FOOTPRINTS IN THE SAND

ONE OF THE PLEASURES OF EXPLORING THE DESERT in Qatar is coming across a dozen or more sets of little footprints in the sand, all quite different, and trying to work out which animal made them and what it was doing at the time. There are the long, narrow slots made by hares, the single lines left by foxes, the alternating claw marks with an undulating line between which are unmistakably lizard, and the strange S-shaped patterns left on the slopes of dunes by sidewinding snakes. Commonest of all are the myriad little footprints left by the patterings of tiny desert rodents, the jerboas, gerbils and jirds.

These little mammals, which are often broadly classified as 'mice' by the non-expert, breed prolifically and this is fortunate, because there can be few animals with more predators. Monitor lizards will crawl down burrows and eat baby rodents, foxes will dig for them, a rodent meal will last a snake a fortnight, and constant danger looms from owls, hawks and other raptors.

Worldwide, there are some 1,700 species of rodents, ranging from large, bulky Indian and African porcupines down to the African Pygmy Mouse, the smallest animal on earth, about the length of your first thumb joint. Of these, about 50 are found throughout the Middle East, with around 20 species inhabiting the Gulf region.

Left: Dunes, SW Qatar. Top: Side-winding track of a viper. Background: Citrullus colocynthis or desert squash. Inset: Baluchistan gerbil

Arnebia hispidissima, the Arabian primrose

HEDGEHOGS

WITHIN A WEEK OR TWO OF ARRIVING IN QATAR FROM BRITAIN IN AUGUST 1985
I encountered a hedgehog in the desert not far from the Salwa Road.
The satisfaction of meeting such a familiar animal was mixed with surprise at seeing it in what seemed an alien environment. I knew nothing about desert animals and had always associated hedgehogs with damp woods, long wet grass and the leaf-strewn bottoms of ditches where they searched for slugs and snails. Yet here was this little fellow, trotting along through bone-dry sand which was almost too hot to touch. It was obvious that my previously-held image of hedgehogs needed updating.

I did not know then that Arabian desert mammals are always smaller than their European counterparts and assumed from its size that it was a juvenile. I now know that it was not a juvenile at all but a full-grown Ethiopian hedgehog (*Paraechinus aethiopicus*). As its name suggests, this species is of African origin and is distributed across the Saharan region from Morocco and into the Arabian peninsula. Unlike the European hedgehog it has a pale band across its face with a darker muzzle and a bald patch on its forehead. The animal

Hedgehog tracks

is light in colour with white-tipped spines, which gives it an overall speckly appearance. The ears are prominent and slightly rounded at the tip.
As in several other species of desert mammals, the large ears of the Ethiopian hedgehog serve to lower its body temperature as blood circulates through the fine capillaries just under the surface of the skin. It has longer legs than European hedgehogs, so that it can raise its body off the sand to allow cooling air to pass underneath.

Since that first happy encounter I have often come across them in the late afternoon, just as evening is drawing in, and at night when driving across the desert. The little animal can put on a surprising turn of speed over a short distance, but its ultimate defence is to curl up into a tight, prickly ball. Not a single part of the body is left unprotected.

Like desert foxes, hedgehogs are omnivorous and this ability to eat almost anything and everything contributes to their survival success. Hedgehogs have almost no enemies except man. Not that they are deliberately killed, but here, as in Europe, many fall victim to speeding cars. Their habit of curling up when danger threatens, which has been a successful method of defence for millions of years, is useless in this new situation.

Ethiopian hedgehog photographed at dusk

A desert hedgehog survives on insects, grubs, wild fruits and seeds and will take young jerboas and gerbils if it can get them. It will also eat the eggs and chicks of ground-nesting birds. In the wadis of the UAE and Oman they will eat frogs and toads, and they are not averse to carrion, no matter how rotten. Wadis and oases where there is plenty of vegetation are the preferred habitat of hedgehogs, although they can survive in the true desert provided there are some plants present. They are often found in date plantations, as well as in gardens and cultivated land on the edge of settlements.

Hedgehogs apparently have no fear of venomous snakes and will attack with all their spines erect. When the unfortunate reptile attempts to bite its predator, all it does is to injure itself on the needle-sharp spikes. The hedgehog waits for an opportunity to seize the snake and kills it by biting through the spine. An unfair contest, but one that gives hedgehogs additional popularity with those who fear snakes. Although not immune to snake bites, hedgehogs have a remarkable tolerance of their venom and are also able to withstand stings from insects such as bees and wasps as well as scorpions.

There are two other species of hedgehog in Arabia: the Long-eared Hedgehog (*Hemiechinus auritus*) and Brandt's Hedgehog (*Paraechinus hypomelas*).

Brandt's Hedgehog, a large, very dark coloured animal, generally prefers a mountain habitat and is unlikely to be found here, but it is just possible that the Long-eared Hedgehog may inhabit Qatar, although it has not yet been recorded. It is rare in the UAE, where it was awarded vulnerable status in 1996, and a single specimen has been recorded in Bahrain.

The Long-eared Hedgehog is smaller than its two relatives. It has longer and more pointed ears than the Ethiopian hedgehog and it lacks the bald patch on its head. In the UAE it inhabits the margins of deserts and is found on cultivated land, where many fall victim to pesticides. It spends the day secreted in a burrow or under a rock, emerging at sunset to spend the night hunting for food. Between dusk and dawn the Long-eared Hedgehog, an agile, fast-moving animal, can cover as much as a kilometre. Hedgehogs have poor vision but good hearing and rely on that and their acute sense of smell to help them locate their prey.

Although the spines of a hedgehog are an excellent defence against any predator, they are poor insulators against the cold, and so, even in Arabia, hedgehogs hibernate during the cooler winter days. They retreat into burrows or into deep clefts between rocks. Hibernation is thought to last for up to six weeks, and the sleeping animal defends itself by remaining tightly curled into a ball with all its spines erect.

Above: Even poisonous snakes like this sand viper are prey for hedgehogs. Right background: Erucaria hispanica in flower. Inset: Brandt's hedgehog

Much has yet to be learned about the distribution and lifecycle of Arabian hedgehogs, but studies show that most produce their young in the hot months of May and June. The average number of babies in each litter is four. The spines, which are soft at birth, soon harden. Surprisingly, hedgehog babies do not open their eyes for about 20 days and so, unlike other small mammals, they remain helpless for a comparatively long period. Gradually the babies begin to feed on solid food, although they will continue to take their mother's milk. By six weeks they are small but fully developed versions of the adult hedgehog. Soon the mother will drive them away, to begin the solitary life of a desert hedgehog.

Silene villosa, the desert campion

H*ARES*

LIKE SEVERAL OF THE OTHER MAMMALS INHABITING QATAR'S DESERT LANDSCAPE, the Cape Hare (*Lepus capensis*) is a smaller version of its European counterpart, the Brown Hare. Perfectly adapted to life in the dry savannah grasslands of East Africa, it also flourishes in all the Arabian Gulf countries and appears to be plentiful in Qatar.

I have seen Cape Hares in every corner of this country, from the great dunes of the far south to the gravel-strewn plains of the north, and also atop the coastal *jebel*, but have probably walked or driven unseeing past many times the number actually sighted. They are remarkably numerous on Saffliyah Island, not far from Doha. When faced with potential danger the hare instinctively crouches and freezes, relying on its perfect camouflage for protection, and will only flee at the last possible moment. This habit makes it hard to make an accurate calculation of the hare population in a given area, because clearly it is not limited to the number actually seen.

On one occasion I was with members of the Natural History Group who were walking across the high plateau at Ras Abrouq, on the west coast, inspecting ancient burial cairns. In the midst of one excavated cairn was a clump of salt-bush and sea-lavender, and as people gathered around it suddenly someone spotted an adult hare crouched in the middle of the bush. Its colour blended perfectly with its background, and it remained motionless, watching us with its wide dark eyes. We moved away to allow the poor creature to recover from its stress.

Like desert foxes and hedgehogs, the Cape Hare, which is also known as the Desert or Arabian Hare, has extra large ears. The relatively small body of the hare is easier to keep cool than a larger frame, and its ears are an efficient cooling system. The hair on its ears is shorter and sparser than on the ears of its European cousin, and this probably helps to expose the skin to the desert breeze. The blood that circulates through thousands of tiny capillaries just below the large surface of the ears is thus cooled before returning to the body.

Cape hare

Being so much smaller than their European cousins, Cape Hares are sometimes mistaken for rabbits, which are not found in Arabia. Unlike rabbits, hares do not dig a burrow. They spend their day in shallow depressions, known as forms, which they dig in the ground or in the wind-blown sandy hummocks that form beside clumps of vegetation. In the summer, as the sun moves across the sky, the hare will change its position, moving to a form on the other side of the bush to obtain maximum shade. In the cooler months hares may not go to the trouble of digging a form, but simply shelter inside a bush, like the hare I described above.

Like the two species of fox that inhabit Qatar and the three-toed Lesser Jerboa, hares have stiff tufts of hair between the pads of their feet, to give a better grip on loose sand. Their soft brown and greyish fur provides perfect camouflage, to help them blend in with their desert background. However, as in rabbits, the underside of the tail is white and this is raised while running, perhaps to act as an alarm signal or to make it easier for young hares to follow their mother at night. In the past, hares were often hunted by the desert-dwelling bedouin and were a valued source of protein. Both falcons and saluki dogs were employed by hunters when after gazelle, but falcons were not generally used for catching hares because the chances of a bird damaging its feathers while fighting to subdue a struggling hare were too great. It was more difficult to catch hares in winter than in summer, because when food was plentiful the animals were very fit and would bolt for safety at the slightest disturbance. In summer, when running wasted valuable energy and water, the hares would try to rely on their camouflage until the last possible moment. A hunter, on his camel, would follow fresh hare tracks until he had located his prey, often crouching among vegetation. Taking his saluki in his arms, he would ride his camel slowly around the area where the hare was hiding, each time coming a little closer. When he was within ten metres or so he would throw the dog towards the bush where the hare was in hiding, causing it to bolt. If the dog failed to catch it within 50 metres the man would call the dog back and go in search of another hare.

Hares when pursued will stop from time to time and sit up with their ears erect, making themselves as visible as possible. A hare can only be caught by a fox or a dog when it is taken by surprise, as given a few seconds' start it can easily outrun its predator, and both animals know this. So when a hare sits and faces its pursuer the signal it is giving is, 'Don't waste your energy. I've seen you.' This avoids a futile chase for both. Hares in Europe and in Qatar behave in exactly the same way, sitting up after the first mad dash to take stock of the enemy and to make clear that they are well beyond pursuit.

Desert hares give birth to an average of two young, known as leverets. Breeding tends to take place during the cooler months. The babies are born fully furred and with their eyes open. Within a few days they leave their birthplace, which may be nothing more than a shallow scrape under a bush and find their own shelter, each remaining within 100m or so of its sibling. This minimises the chances of an entire litter being wiped out by a predator such as a fox. The mother visits each baby regularly to let it suckle, but young hares are able to eat grass and shrubs almost as soon as they are born. They quickly become independent of the mother, which helps to increase their chance of survival should the mother be killed. At 8 months they are sexually mature.

Cape hare

What of the future of the Cape Hare in this country? The main danger is, inevitably, loss of habitat, and in addition many die under the wheels of traffic. But on the other hand, cultivated land, vegetable gardens and the great stretches of green grass of the golf course at West Bay are irresistible to hares, so while human disturbance of the landscape is infringing on their natural habitat, at the same time they are being provided with a source of high-quality nutrition. Hares, despite their shy and solitary nature, are able to adapt quite well to life in a landscape that has been extensively altered by human activity.

A survey that took place in the 1980s in the UAE revealed that ticks brought to the desert on imported livestock weakened hares so much that they could no longer out-run their chief predator, the fox. That might also be the case here. However, hares are resilient animals. There are still areas of desert in Qatar that are rarely frequented either by humans or their livestock and it seems likely that the Cape Hare will continue to survive here in the foreseeable future

MANY TERRESTRIAL REPTILES HAVE SUCCESSFULLY ADAPTED TO THE HARSH CLIMATE of sandy and rocky deserts. Their scaly skin, which is regularly renewed, helps to prevent them from dehydrating in arid environments. Their main limitation is their reliance on external heat: reptiles cannot control their own body temperature and require a level of around 25-30° C before they become fully mobile active.

In Qatar, with its high summer temperatures and warm winters, reaching the required temperature is rarely a problem, but reptiles also have to ensure that they do not overheat. For this reason many species leave their burrows or hiding places under rocks or in deep sand only in the early morning and late afternoon. Some are entirely nocturnal.

Among the reptiles of the Qatar desert are several species of snakes. Many people on first coming to Qatar wonder about the risk of encountering poisonous snakes when out camping at weekends. In fact, the danger is very small. Of the nine species of land snake that may be present in the peninsula, only one is poisonous. Two others are mildly poisonous and the others are completely harmless to people. Some species are positively beneficial, as they help to keep down the rodent population in settled areas.

The rear-fanged sand snake Psammophis schokari

Harmless snakes have short teeth solidly embedded in their jaws. As they have no poison glands, the purpose of the teeth is simply to enable the snake to keep a grip on its prey. In addition to short teeth, mildly poisonous snakes have one or more pairs of slightly longer grooved fangs, through which venom trickles into the wounded prey. They are sometimes called 'rear-fanged', as the fangs are located to the rear of the mouth and are only used when the reptile wishes to subdue its prey before swallowing. Since the fangs are not used for biting, people are in little or no danger from a mildly poisonous snake.

Another group of snakes has long erectile fangs, which hinge back when not in use. In fact, they are so long that the snake cannot close its mouth when the fangs are erect. These long teeth allow the snake to inflict a deep wound into which they inject a large quantity of venom. In Qatar the only representative of this group is the Horned Viper (*Cerastes cerastes gasperetti*) also known as the Sand Viper, which is found throughout the Arabian peninsula and eastwards to Iran. It is a short, rather thick snake, reaching a length of approximately 80 cm., and is light brown with cream and darker brown markings. There is a distinctive dark stripe through the eye and a small projection, the 'horn', over each. Some have no horns, and in Egypt snake-charmers are reputed to remedy the deficiency by driving a couple of hedgehog spines

through the snake's upper jaw! When moving over loose sand, the Horned Viper achieves minimum contact with the surface by 'side-winding', a movement in which only two points of the body are in contact with the ground at any time. It is this movement that leaves the curious pattern of parallel S-shaped tracks that is often found in soft sand or on the sides of dunes. All 'side-winders' resume their normal sinuous movements when on firm ground.

Horned Vipers are not aggressive snakes and, although they commonly bury themselves just under the sand, the thudding of approaching feet gives them plenty of time to disappear. If approached, they rub their scales together to make a loud 'hissing' sound. A few years ago an expatriate woman who was picnicking in the 'singing dunes' area of Qatar, near Mesaieed was bitten because she put her hand under a rock beneath which a Horned Viper was sheltering. She made a full recovery.

The venom of vipers is haemotoxic, causing bleeding in internal organs and kidney failure. The average person is highly unlikely to encounter a viper in Qatar, unless they spend much time in the desert, as these venomous snakes stay well clear of settled areas. In twenty years of walking the deserts of Qatar I have never seen a Horned Viper, although I have often come across its side-winding tracks. Although they are generally nocturnal, one was recently photographed coiled up on a path at Ras Laffan in broad daylight.

In neighbouring UAE the most common poisonous snake is the Saw-scaled Viper (*Echis carinatus*), which is found both in sandy deserts and in the mountains. Its bite is extremely poisonous and recovery from it is often both long and painful. A rarer relative, the Carpet Viper (*Echis coloratus*), equally venomous, occurs in the mountains. Although a comprehensive survey of the reptiles of Qatar has not yet been made, it is thought to be very unlikely that the Saw-scaled Viper occurs here.

A reptile you are more likely to come across is the Rat Snake (*Coluber ventromaculatus*), which can reach almost a metre in length and is sandy-coloured with dark brown markings. Rat snakes are active during the day and will climb trees in search of small birds, to vary their diet of reptiles and rodents. It may turn up in your garden, and has alarmed many a Doha householder, quite unnecessarily! Some years ago the British

Top: Cerastes gasperetti, the Horned viper
Bottom: print of sand viper's body left in the sand

ambassador to Qatar noticed, from an upstairs window, what appeared to be
a length of thin rope dangling from a tree in the embassy garden.
While he was looking it, it
dropped to the
ground and
slithered
away

Above: Rat snake (Coluber ventromaculatus)
Below: False cobra (Malpolon moilensis)

Another snake commonly seen in the daytime is the z, which can
reach a length of 1.5 metres. It is sometimes seen in Doha gardens. I have
encountered Sand Snakes sunning themselves on jebel outcrops on the north-east coast and among the
ruins of the old north-western city of Al Zubara. Sand Snakes are mildly poisonous, but are highly unlikely
to give a human a venomous bite.

Once, at Al Zubara, a startled Sand Snake streaked away from us along a wall and into a crevice. Almost
instantaneously a lizard shot out like a cork from a popgun, sailing right into the air in its panic. It looked
comical, although of course a matter of life and death for the lizard.

Sand Snakes are slim and fast-moving. They are dark grey or olive brown with black and white lines at the
side of the head. Some have longitudinal stripes along the whole of their body. Being a snake that is out
and about during the day, it has round pupils in its eyes, which are a conspicuous red colour. Nocturnal
snakes have pupils that narrow into slits in daylight. They are the longest of all the Arabian snakes,
reaching a length of approximately 1.50 metres. If you see a long, thin, dark-coloured ribbon streaking
away from you when you are out walking, it is probably a Sand Snake.

From time to time there are reports of people claiming to have come across cobras in the desert. What
they are seeing is probably the Hooded Malpolon (*Malpolon moilensis*) which is sometimes called the False
Cobra. If alarmed it will rear up and hiss and spread the skin of its neck in a cobra-like manner. The
Hooded Malpolon is another diurnal snake and has yellow eyes with round black pupils. It is a light, sandy
brown with a pattern of darker brown spots. It inhabits the gravel plains in the centre and north of Qatar,
and prefers areas where there is some vegetation, so it is not found in the areas of sand dunes to the
south of the country. Like the Sand Snake, the Hooded Malpolon is mildly toxic, but with its poison fangs
at the very back of its mouth it is very unlikely to cause harm to a human.

Capparis spinosa - the caper plant

DESERT SUN-WORSHIPPERS

ANYONE DRIVING ALONG SMALLER ROADS THROUGH QATAR'S DESERT LANDSCAPE WILL have noticed large lizards sunning themselves on the warm tarmac or, if they have any sense, streaking for their burrows at the sound of the approaching vehicle. All too often, the ones that leave it too late end up as road-kill.

These are the Spiny-tailed Agamas (*Uromastyx aegyptia microlepis*), known as *dhub* in Arabic. They are the second-largest lizard in Qatar and present a fearsome appearance, with their heavy, spiked tails and sharp claws. They look more like something out of Jurassic Park than any other local reptile I can think of, but they are, in fact, harmless herbivores. If cornered, they lash out strongly with their armoured tails and are capable of giving a nasty bite, although their strong jaws have no teeth. The naturalist and writer Marijcke Jongbloed, who was based in the UAE for 20 years, had a passion for *dhubs* and occasionally handled them, but I have always kept a respectful distance!

Dhubs can grow to a length of 65cm and live in burrows in a colony. Each burrow has an entrance twice as wide as it is high, with a convex top and level floor. The burrows are normally about 20 to 50 metres apart, with as many as thirty or forty individuals inhabiting each colony. It is possible that more than one *dhub* inhabits each burrow, which may extend downwards as much as two metres. These colonies occur all over Qatar, but seem to be most common on the central gravel plain, although they also inhabit sandier areas and are present on the small island in the bay of Al Khor. We often see *dhubs* on the road between Al Wakra and Umm Bab and also in the area around Al Zubara in the north-west.

An active *dhub* colony can be quickly spotted by the droppings scattered around: they consist of large, elongated dry pellets, followed by a drop of white urea and, on fresh droppings, a blob of orange jelly lubricant. This quickly evaporates in the heat. Adult *dhubs* are herbivores, but the young lizards may occasionally eat small lizards or insects to obtain protein, if the opportunity offers.

These lizards never drink water; obtaining all the moisture they need from their food plants. They have a gland near the anus which extracts all the liquid from the faeces and recirculates it within the body, while a special gland in the nostrils separates the salts and discharges them.

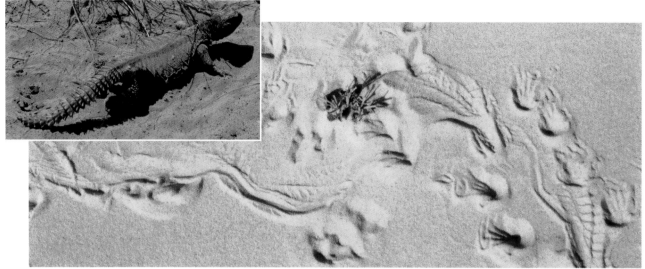

Dhub track. Inset: Spiny-tailed Agama

The *dhub* is the only lizard in Qatar which is strictly vegetarian; all the others are insect-eaters, with the exception of the Desert Monitor which takes larger prey. Like all reptiles, lizards and geckos regulate their body temperature by adapting it to the ambient air temperature. They only become active when they have warmed up. The terrain of Qatar, with its warm and dry climate, provides ideal conditions for this. In fact, in order not to overheat, many species have become nocturnal and are rarely seen.

Dhubs hibernate during the cooler winter months and become more active from March onwards. When a *dhub* emerges from its burrow, it sits at the entrance to warm up. To begin with its colour is slate-grey all over, but as the sun's rays take effect it becomes a mottled yellow. The face has an ancient look about it, like that of an elderly tortoise, and the large eyes are a deep amber hue. The heavily folded skin on the neck and body allows the animal to inflate itself with air when threatened. If cornered by a would-be predator, such as a bird of prey or a Desert Monitor, a *dhub* will inflate the loose skin that lies in folds around its neck and body to make itself look bigger and strike out with its spiny tail. It will also hiss loudly to create an impression of aggressiveness. But *dhubs* generally rely on their speed and make a dash for their burrows if alarmed. Their principal enemy used to be humans, as the roasted tail of a *dhub* was formerly a popular dish among the tent-dwelling bedouin and is still considered a delicacy by some people. It has a reputation as an aphrodisiac!

The usual method of catching them is to place a long, narrow, nail-studded piece of wood with loops of fishing line attached to it besides the food plants near a burrow. The *dhub* gets entangled in the loops and when it dives into its burrow the piece of wood jams against the entrance, preventing it from reaching the depths of the burrow. It can then be hauled out by means of the fishing line. They can sometimes be seen for sale in the pet souq, which is sad, because they are almost impossible to keep alive in captivity, refusing to eat and dying of starvation and stress.

The size of *dhub* populations is directly related to heavy rainfall which has an effect on the plants on which they feed. The plentiful rain of 2005 will probably result in an increase in the *dhub* population over that of the past few years when the rainfall was less.

Another, even larger lizard which inhabits Qatar is the grey Desert Monitor (*Varanus griseus*). The Arabian name for it is *wirral*. Reaching a maximum length of 1.2 m, it has a back and tail banded with stripes of a dark colour, interspersed with lighter spots, and a long tail tapering to a thin point.

Desert Monitor - Varanus griseus

Interestingly, the name *wirral* means the same as the English name Monitor. Presumably the reptile got its name from the concentrated expression it appears to wear.

Like all Monitors, this lizard is a carnivorous hunter and eater of carrion. It will also take the eggs and young of other reptiles and of ground-nesting and tree-nesting birds alike. It will dig for its prey and is reported to be cannibalistic. It has strong, sharp teeth and swallows its food whole. The roof of its mouth is made of thick bone to prevent damage to the brain by large mouthfuls of prey. Monitors are solitary animals, unlike *dhubs*, and each requires a wide area of territory.

In the 1980s we occasionally saw Monitors on the central gravel plain, but nowhere else, so I suspect that they are less common and less widespread than *dhubs*. Environmental officers at Ras Laffan report that they are present within the large fenced area around the industrial complex. The last time I saw a Monitor lizard was about ten years ago, and it may be that their numbers are declining.

An attractive little lizard to be found living in the great sand dunes of southern Qatar is the Sand Skink (*Scincus mitranus*). It is commonly known as the 'Sand Fish' because of its ability to dive beneath the surface of the sand in a fraction of a second and then 'swim' underneath it, showing no trace on the surface. Beautifully marked, with a glossy skin like glazed porcelain and a row of rectangular dark spots on its flanks, it is a relative of the Ocellated or Garden Skink (*Chalcides ocellatus*), rather darker in colour, which inhabits Doha gardens. Once, we watched some herdsmen from a camel camp nab a sand fish on a 'singing dune' near the old road to Messai'eed; they assured us it had a 'very good taste'.

The Sand Fish - Scincus mitranus

We took their word for it! Later, we managed to catch one ourselves, down at Khor Al Adaid, and photograph it. We released it on the sand and then tried to recapture it, but the Sand Fish had instantly vanished.

A similar lizard, which is less common here, is *Scincus scincus conirostris*. It looks, to the amateur eye, almost identical to the Sand Skink except for the absence of the dark spots on its sides.

A small lizard which inhabits the central gravel plain of Qatar is the Yellow-spotted or Blue-headed Agama (*Trapelus flavimaculatus*). I have seen many during the past few years. Adults measure up to 20cm in length. Brown, with mottled lighter markings, the Toad-head has long legs in comparison with the length of its body, and if feeling threatened will rear up and hiss with its mouth open. It gets its name 'Blue-headed' from the colour-change it undergoes when alarmed or excited - the head then becomes deep blue and the tail orange.

In soft sand, and particularly on sand dunes, you are more likely to encounter its relative, the Arabian Toad-headed or Yellow Toad-headed Agama (*Phrynocephalus arabicus*). Adapted to life in the sand, this small lizard has fringes of scales as eyelashes to keep sand grains out of its eyes. Its body colour varies to match its environment: the Toad-headed Agamas of the pale golden sands of Qatar being

Blue-headed Agama

Arabian Toad-headed agama - Phrynocephalus arabicus

much lighter than those inhabiting the red sand dunes found inland in the UAE. The markings are black and white, with yellow patches on top of the head. On the underside of the tail is a black tip, used for signalling, which is highly visible when the lizard raises and curls its tail.

The Toad-headed Agama has long legs, and uses them to raise its body above the sand surface on very hot days. It will stand poised and motionless for minutes on end while looking for prey, and then suddenly dart at an insect. When threatened, this lizard can sink vertically into the sand in a split second by rapidly vibrating its body, a process that has been nick-named 'shimmy burial'.

Away from the gravel plain, among the rocky areas of coastal *jebel*, tiny lizards dart at lightning speed, zipping under a bush or rock when danger threatens. These are Dwarf Rock Geckos (*Pristurus rupestris*), delicately made little creatures with long tails and mottled brown coloration that provides perfect camouflage. In fact, if they stayed still they would probably remain unseen, but that is not the way of these geckos. Their feet have long, thin, finger-like toes, typical of geckos. Dwarf Rock Geckos have a number of signals that they can make with their tails, ranging from submission and appeasement to threat and aggression, hence their alternative name of Rock Semaphore Geckos.

Anyone living in Qatar, whether they go out exploring in the desert or prefer to stay closer to home, is bound to encounter the Yellow-bellied House Gecko (*Hemidactylus flaviviridus)*. In Indonesia a similar species of house-dwelling lizard is known as ' tjitjak', and that exactly describes the chacking noise they make, like two pebbles being knocked together, during the summer breeding season. Geckos are, apparently, the only lizards in Qatar with vocal chords. In June their eggs appear, like tiny oval white capsules, tucked into crevices in

floors and walls around the house. The harmless House Geckos do a good job catching cockroaches, mosquitoes and other insect pests, so it is a pity they are considered poisonous by some local people. A similar but much smaller house gecko is the Turkish gecko (*Hemidactylus turcicus*), which also has vocal cords.

For anyone interested in learning more about the reptilian inhabitants of the Qatar desert, the months of March, April and May are the ideal time to go lizard spotting. Cool weather keeps them 'indoors', but once the temperature begins to rise, and plants and insects are abundant, the reptiles are out and about and, like all of us, enjoying the sunshine.

Yellow--bellied House Gecko

SURPRISINGLY, THERE ARE PEOPLE WHO LIVE FOR YEARS IN DOHA WITHOUT EVER SETTING foot in the open desert, which they are convinced is full of hidden dangers. Some years ago our neighbours solemnly cautioned us about quick sands! They warned us that if we went off-road our vehicle would be in danger of being swallowed up. It was clear that they did not believe our assurances that no such terrors exist here.

One perceived hazard which worries some newcomers is the possibility of being stung by a scorpion. Scorpions are found here, as they are in all but the colder regions of the world, but being mainly nocturnal they are rarely seen during the day. Still, everyone knows what a scorpion looks like even if they have never seen one. Their highly distinctive body shape seems ingrained in our minds from earliest times and conjures up images of an evil-intentioned, aggressive little creature scuttling around and lashing out with its tail in all directions. However, in common with other venomous creatures, scorpions avoid humans and will only sting when threatened. They hide under rocks and in clumps of vegetation, but what they really seem to prefer are pieces of old rotten wood, metal or even expanded polystyrene, of which, alas, there is no shortage even in the remotest areas. Once, when we were camping, we threw a big piece of driftwood on to the bonfire and a scorpion ran out and over someone's bare toes. It was a reminder to us that one should always wear closed shoes, not sandals or flip-flops, when walking around after dark.

Although scorpions have a reputation as dangerous killers, it is largely undeserved. As with snakes, another perceived desert hazard, many species are harmless. Some are mildly toxic and only a very small minority can give stings that require medical attention. Even with the most venomous species, the sting is only likely to prove fatal to children, the elderly and those with an impaired immune system.

Calligonum comosum, or 'arta' - typical shelter for scorpions

equipment, you don't know what may have crawled under them or into them during the night. Always shake out your shoes in the morning before putting them on.

In the unfortunate event of a sting, reassure the victim, clean the wound and apply a firm supporting bandage but not a tourniquet. Keep the site of the sting as cool as possible, using crushed ice if available. It must be kept below the level of the heart. In hospital a local anaesthetic will be administered by injection to relieve the pain, followed by an oral analgesic. The injured person is normally kept in for observation for six hours and then discharged if no deterioration in his or her condition occurs.

CAMEL SPIDERS

CAMEL SPIDERS OR SUN SPIDERS, ALSO KNOWN AS WIND SCORPIONS BECAUSE OF THEIR speed, are voracious eaters with enormous appetites. They eat any living thing they can catch – insects, desert rodents, lizards, snakes and even small birds. Some people believe that they also eat humans…but more of that later.

Their speed and aggressiveness make camel spiders fearsome hunters, and ounce for ounce their body-crunching jaws deliver one of the most powerful bites in the animal kingdom. Using their massive jaws like a combination of pincers and knives, they chew their victims into pulp and then exude an enzyme that digests the flesh, before sucking it into their stomachs.

Camel spiders are not true spiders, as they belong to a large order called *solfugida* which numbers around 1000 species. As members of the arachnid family they are related to spiders, scorpions, mites and ticks. They appear to have ten legs, but the first pair actually consists of pedipalps (leg-like appendages of the mouth parts) - used as sensory organs in feeding, fighting and mating. They also have a sensory organ underneath their abdomen - a very peculiar structure of two rows of racket organs, called malleoli, found nowhere else in the animal world. With this they feel for vibrations in the ground which tell them whether a prey or a predator is approaching.

Camel spiders hide under rocks or in their burrows during the day, emerging at night on their high-speed hunting missions. In fact the name *solfugida* means 'avoiding the sun.'

On one occasion we were camping at the side of a dry, rocky wadi in Ras al Khaimah, UAE. Soon after sunset in the light of our camp fire the ground seemed to ripple with movement as scores of camel spiders raced around, the shadows cast by their bulky bodies and long, jointed legs making them seem even bigger and scarier than they were. We made very sure that the fly-screen on our tent was securely fastened!

Camel spiders are not so common in Qatar as in the Emirates, but nevertheless they do exist here and are occasionally seen by desert campers. Their legs are covered with short, stiff hairs, which help traction as they race around. The species found in this region is a light reddish-brown. Their bite is non-poisonous, but they

Left: Convolvulus deserti Above: Camel spider

are capable of giving anyone who disturbs them a nasty nip. The great Arabian traveller Wilfred Thesiger described in *Arabian Sands*, the account of his crossing of the Empty Quarter, the horror with which these fast-moving creatures filled him: 'They were common in all but the most arid places. They were as much as three inches across, with hairy, reddish legs, and pendulous bodies, and they scuttled about in the firelight.'

Three of the ten known families of camel spider have been identified in Abu Dhabi: *Galeodidae*, *Solpugidae* and *Rhagodidae*. No study of camel spiders in Qatar has yet been undertaken, but it seems likely that at least one of these families is present here. *Galeodidae* and *Solpugidae* are both long-legged with sandy-coloured bodies, whereas the *Rhagodidae* are smaller and darker coloured.

Not only are camel spiders ferocious predators, they are equally violent in their relations with each other. Males risk being killed and eaten when approaching a female to mate. If mating is accomplished the female will lay between 50 and 200 eggs in a burrow, and will feed the young with prey until they can hunt independently, but young camel spiders have been known to kill and eat each other.

Among the nomadic, tent-dwelling peoples of the Middle East, camel spiders are reputed to creep up on sleepers, inject them with a powerful anaesthetic and eat their fill. A few years ago a British nurse in Qatar who had worked in Abu Dhabi told me of a bedouin woman and her baby who had been brought to hospital with fearsome wounds, attributed to a camel spider. The woman had had part of her face eaten away, and the poor baby had bled to death after a vein in its neck was severed. The nurse believed that the injuries were the result of camel spider attack, having heard of other instances while in the UAE. When consulted about this, an entomologist said that the bites were almost certainly made by rats, although it seems rather unlikely that a person would continue sleeping while a rat was biting them. I have also heard reports of workers on a desert construction site in Saudi Arabia who slept under their vehicles when it was cold, in order to benefit from the residual warmth of the engine. They would sometimes wake in the morning with wounds which they attributed to camel spiders. The experts assure us that such stories belong strictly to the realms of folklore. Unfortunately these bedouin old wives' tales received a new lease of life from American soldiers who fought in the Gulf War of 1991 and took part in the invasion of Iraq in 2003. A photo posted on a popular website showed a soldier holding up a couple of camel spiders which appeared to be the size of lobsters. It was the camera angle which made them appear so large, but the picture received wide publicity in the United States, and the tale that camel spiders anaesthetize their human victims before eating them was repeated more than once by ill-informed narrators of TV documentaries.

Sensory organs, called malleoli, underneath the abdomen of a camel spider

Other popular stories were that camel spiders grow to the size of dinner plates, and race across the desert making a high screaming noise as they run. When not dining off the American infantry they were said to feed on the stomachs of camels – some rumours even held that they did it from the inside!

Of course the size of the spiders was grossly exaggerated, but all the same they can reach impressive dimensions. One website states that they average about 2.75 inches (70 mm) in length. However, when I was living in northern Nigeria we managed to catch one and confine it in a glass tank. We measured it, and from the tips of its jaws to the rear end of its body it was 7.5 inches (190 mm) long.

THE MANGROVE FORESTS

AROUND AL KHOR AND AL THAKHIRA, ON THE NORTH-EAST COAST OF QATAR, THE coast is fringed with forests of mangroves, interspersed with shallow tidal creeks. The thick, grey-green foliage of the trees forms a clear dividing line between the pale yellow salt marshes which fringe the shore and the deep blue of the sea and sky. Home to a host of creatures of all kinds, mangroves are, ecologically, among the most important vegetation in the country.

Qatar has only one species of mangrove, *Avicennia marina*, sometimes called the Grey Mangrove to distinguish it from other species with darker leaves. Worldwide there are almost 50 species of mangroves. *Avicennia marina,* called *gurm* in Arabic, is the most widely distributed of all the species. Mangroves are tropical trees and generally will not survive where average temperatures fall below 19 C, although one species is know to exist in New Zealand on sites where the temperature occasionally drops below zero.
The mangrove is a very tough plant, capable of tolerating extreme conditions, which is demonstrated by its

Mangroves at Al Thakhira

existence here and in the UAE, where the seawater on average has three times the salt content of seawater elsewhere. However, the energy required for the plant to excrete salt stunts its growth, hence the somewhat dwarfed appearance of the local trees. Salt crystals can be seen thickly coating the undersides of the leaves.

At Al Khor and Al Thakhira, the areas immediately inland from the mangroves are often flooded and turn into wet and muddy salt marshes. These are home to other salt-tolerant species of plants known as halophytes, including the widespread succulent *Halocnemum strobilaceum* and the dense shrubs of *Arthrocnemum macrostachyum*.

The salt flats are popular recreational areas for bird watchers, kite fliers and for people taking the dog for a run at weekends. To them the mangroves may appear simply as a group of trees on the seashore, without

their importance as key elements in a complex ecological system being realised. Mangroves are extremely beneficial, not only in stabilising the coast line but also in providing the initial link in the food chain of organisms which nourishes the inhabitants of the intertidal zones.

The algae cover of the mud flats between the mangroves assists in binding together the mud particles, but cracks and dries when exposed to the sun by low tide. When high tides wash over it is rejuvenated. The pale, creamy colour of the mud itself is determined by diatoms, minute organisms which release oxygen.

The substrate of the mangrove habitat is heavy silt, rich with rotting organic material. It is virtually anaerobic, i.e. it contains very little oxygen, and anyone who wades into the waterlogged mud between the trees will notice a strong, sulphur-like smell as their boots disturb the ground. This is hydrogen sulphide, which is produced by bacteria that exist without light or oxygen. Mangroves have evolved a specialised system to cope with the anaerobic conditions. Aerial roots called pneumatophores poke up above the mud and water surface to allow the plant to breathe and are connected with the main root system which anchors the tree into the ground. From a mature tree long lines of pneumatophores can be seen radiating in all directions.

Young mangroves surrounded by pneumatophores   Inset: Mangrove flower

A further specialised mechanism enables seeds to germinate in the saline and anaerobic conditions. Seeds falling into the mud would suffocate without oxygen, so the tree solves the problem by being viviparous: producing seeds that germinate while still attached to the parent plant. The tiny plant receives water and nutrients from its parent and continues to grow until the weight of the seedling causes it to fall into the mud beneath the tree. Even if covered with water, seedlings are able to withstand long periods of inundation. Some continue to grow near the parent tree, trapped in the web of pneumatophores, while others are carried by the tides to new sites.

The complex webs of pneumatophores and root systems surrounding the mangrove stands restrict tidal flow and thus cause a build up of silt. Gradually a new muddy coastal habitat is established, encouraging the development of other plants. The build up of mud continues, and the coastal area becomes stabilised. Other marine organisms then develop within the habitat.

To have some idea of just how complex and fascinating is the ecology of mangroves, one needs to brave the muddy conditions and wade in among the trees. Great care is needed to avoid damaging the lines of aerial roots, and stout boots are necessary: accidentally stepping on a spiky root can be painful, but only then can one observe at close quarters the small creatures living among the roots and the myriad of insects feeding on the flowers. The thick leaf-cover and stout branches provide ideal cover for nesting birds. Small crabs inhabiting the muddy flats and the banks of the channels help to remove rotting organic matter, including the fallen mangrove leaves, and their burrows help to aerate the waterlogged ground. The flowers of the mangroves are a rich source of nectar for insects such as bees, which make their nests among the branches. The shallow waters are a haven for small fish during their juvenile years until they are big enough to survive in the open sea. These include commercial varieties of fish.

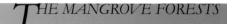

Oil pollution is clearly a hazard for mangroves, as even a thin film of oil on the spiky aerial roots can suffocate the trees. Another danger is over-grazing by camels. Camels enjoy munching on the salty leaves, and it used to be a popular belief among the bedouin that eating mangrove leaves made camels very strong and able to undertake long migrations.

The vital difference an established mangrove ecosystem can make to a coast line was borne home to the world by the effect of the tsunami of December 2004 on the coast of Thailand. Since 1960 over half the mangrove forests of Thailand have been cleared away to make room for intensive fish farming or tourism-related development. Many of these areas were devastated by the tsunami, whereas villages protected by the remaining mangroves escaped major damage and loss of life.

The mangroves of Al Khor and Al Thakhira are home to a wide variety of birds.
A good site for bird watching is the causeway leading to the small island known as Jazirat bin Ghanim in the bay of Khor Shaqiq. Here both the White-breasted Kingfisher and the Common Kingfisher can be seen during the winter months, their brilliant plumage flashing like a streak of brilliant iridescent blue against the green of the mangroves. Greater Flamingoes pick their way among the wider stretches of open water, and Western Reef Herons and Little Egrets stand patiently in the shallows. The haunting cries of Curlew Sandpipers and Redshanks echo over the forest, and above the fishing, squabbling and calling shore birds circle the watchful Marsh Harriers.

In days gone by mangrove wood was much in use for a variety of purposes: the poles which support the flat roofs of traditional stone-built houses, parts of furniture, the struts of boats, and above all for the production of charcoal. Large piles of mangrove branches would be gathered and covered with a thick layer of sand and ashes. This was then fired and left to slowly smoulder. The combustion process lasted as long as a week and the resulting charcoal was used by local people for cooking and traded to other regions where the wood was not available. Excavations in the 1980s and in 2000 on Jazirat Bin Ghanim revealed ancient hearths containing traces of charcoal, and carbon dating of the charcoal has proved that the mangrove plantations of the north-eastern coast have been established for at least four thousand years.

Mangroves surrounding Jazirat bin Ghanim   Inset: Mangrove fruit

A desert palette of salt-bushes: *Halocnemum strobilaceum* (foreground),
Halopeplis perfoliata (background left) and *Zygophyllum qatarense* (background right)

Breeding ground of Socotra Cormorants, immature birds pale-coloured

ANYONE FAMILIAR WITH THE COASTLINE OF QATAR WILL HAVE NOTICED LONG, WAVERING strings of dark-coloured birds flying fast and low over the water, or drifting in dense flocks which constantly change shape like puffs of smoke as they move. These are Socotra Cormorants (*Phalacrocorax nigrogularis*), known as *lohar* in local Arabic.

Unique in being the only bird species endemic to the Arabian region, they are intensely social creatures, and can easily be distinguished from the Great Cormorants which visit our shores in the winter months. Great Cormorants can be seen perched on buoys and fishing boats in local harbours and on the floating rubber booms around the Gulf Marina.

The Great Cormorant is an altogether larger and heavier bird, with white patches on the head and neck and a jaunty orange bib on the throat. Socotra Cormorants are slimmer and more streamlined, with very dark plumage, iridescent in sunlight, and are built for fast flying and, above all, diving. It has been officially recorded that these cormorants can dive to a depth of 18 metres. Unofficially, that depth was verified by a commercial diver who worked for some years in Qatari waters. He was finning along a pipe-line at 18 metres when he received a sudden and painful blow to the head. Thinking his last moment had come, he looked up to see a Socotra Cormorant swimming away from him! During their dives for fish, inevitably, some birds get entangled in nets or caught in fish traps and drown.

The cormorants we see around the Qatar peninsula almost certainly all come from the great nesting sites on Suwad al Janubiyah, a small, flat, sandy island with sparse vegetation, clearly visible from Ras Abrouq on the west coast of Qatar. It forms part of the Huwar Islands archipelago. In the winter of 2002-3, more than 24,500 breeding pairs congregated in two nesting areas on this island, each pair laying an average of two large bluish-white eggs in a circular scrape on the rocky ground. These two areas contain an estimated 10% or more of the total breeding population of 220,000 pairs throughout Arabian waters.

Extremely sensitive to human pressure, over the last 30 years 12 colonies have become extinct around the Gulf as sites have been encroached upon by development or subjected to prolonged human disturbance. Today only 13 breeding colonies remain, of which the colony on the island of Suwad al Janubiyah is the largest. Suwad means 'blackness' in Arabic, an echo perhaps from the days when the entire island was covered with breeding birds.

In January 2003 I joined a team from UNESCO, which was carrying out a survey on the Huwar Islands. The boat I was travelling on passed to windward of the cormorant colony. The smell was truly fearsome, inevitable when nearly 50,000 fish-eating birds congregate in a small area. Wherever one looked the sky was full of the black, drifting skeins, clouds and trailing wisps of cormorants skimming over the waves.

On the island the birds are packed as tightly together as a penguin rookery. Fights and squabbles are unavoidable, and the predatory Yellow-legged Gulls are ever on the watch for unguarded eggs or chicks. The chicks retain their grey-white juvenile plumage for some months, and once mobile they form large standing creches, which are watched over by adult birds while others fly off to fish.

Seeing them in such numbers, it is hard to realize that they are in fact an endangered species, but it is estimated that the total world population now numbers less than half a million, with approximately 110,000 breeding pairs. The UNESCO team found unmistakeable signs that the colony had been robbed of eggs by people coming by boat, bringing a wheelbarrow with them to transport the eggs from the nesting ground.

The breeding population on Suwad al Janubiyah is down from the 1994-8 estimate of an average 26,000 nests per year, and the population is still affected by a disaster that occurred in November 1997, when heavy rain flooded the whole colony, chilling incubated eggs, drowning chicks by the thousand and leaving thousands more to die from hypothermia.

In April 2003, at the end of the breeding season, the population suffered a further catastrophe when a thunderstorm accompanied by strong winds killed large numbers of half-grown chicks.

The breeding season begins in September when the first eggs are laid, and lasts until April when the young are strong enough to fly. Once the season is over the Huwar Islands cormorants disperse around the Gulf of Salwa, including the coastal waters of Qatar.

Unlike the more solitary Great Cormorants, the Socotra Cormorants are comfortable in a crowd, and this is demonstrated by their roosting procedure. They congregate in dense flocks in isolated locations, among them the western shores of off-shore islands lying between Bahrain, Saudi Arabia and the Rubuds, the two most northerly islets of the Hawar archipelago. The birds cram tightly together, shoulder to shoulder, even though plenty of space is available. The reason for this behaviour is not fully understood, but experts theorize that it may be to provide shade for their feet when temperatures can exceed 60° C. In August 2002 a roost of 30,000 birds was recorded on the island of Umm Nassan.

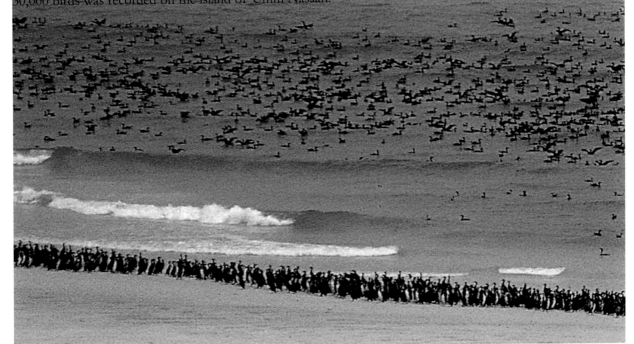

Sometimes, during calm weather, the cormorants will form a floating roost out at sea, a 'raft' of birds as tightly packed as on land. They drift for hours along tidal streams or currents.

During the hottest months there is almost total inactivity between dawn and mid-afternoon, when the day's fishing expeditions begin. A common activity pattern is for a group of birds to fly out from the back of an onshore roost and drop into the sea in front of the mass of birds along the water front, triggering them to swim out or fly to join their fellows. More and more birds enter the water, until the entire roost is drifting seawards on the current.

The first thing that cormorants do when they leave the land is to bathe, a lengthy and thorough procedure. The feet are used to scratch at the breast feathers to dislodge dirt and parasites. The birds then repeatedly duck their heads underwater and beat their wings against the surface of the sea to throw water over their backs. The wings are then outstretched to dry, followed by preening.

The flock then embarks on a fishing foray, flying along a selected route, each bird watching intently for signs of shoals. As soon as fish are sighted the forward movement comes to a sudden stop, as the birds splash down on the water. Cormorants always dive from a floating position, like ducks.

Adult Socotra cormorant

Birds which have caught a fish often fly a short distance from the flock to avoid being robbed while they swallow their prey.

The continuous rolling movement of a flock of Socotra Cormorants, as some birds dive while others rise and fly off before returning to the fishing frenzy, was first commented on and recorded by the explorer and naturalist Robert Cheesman on his journey to Salwa in 1921.

The formation of a flock of birds in flight varies according to the activity. A departure for fishing involves the simultaneous movement of an entire flock, a dense sheet of birds flying just above the sea surface. The birds move en masse without a leader, and the front of the flock can be hundreds of metres wide. But when fishing comes to an end and groups of birds break off their activities to head for home, they form the familiar long, wavering, V-shaped skeins or undulating strings. A flock will often make a trip of close to 100 km to their fishing grounds and back.

The decline of the population in Qatar of Socotra Cormorants may in part be due to the floods of 1997 and 2003, although over-fishing in the Gulf by humans will also inevitably affect their numbers. Disturbance of the breeding sites and theft of eggs are another threat to their existence.

It remains to be seen whether, given time, the population will recover.

OSPREYS

ONE OF THE MOST SPECTACULAR BIRDS FREQUENTING THE COASTLINE OF QATAR IS the osprey (*Pandion haliaetus*). Although in many parts of the world it is endangered by egg collectors, or by fishermen who regard it as a competitor, in Qatar it is relatively common. Ospreys can be observed from the Corniches in Doha and Al Khor and near coastal villages, as well as on the remote coasts of northern Qatar and in the far south.

On the Huwar Islands archipelago, located off the north-west coast of the Qatar peninsula, 20 pairs of ospreys nested in 1998/9, and a total of 47 birds were in residence. Sometimes two pairs will occupy one small island. These birds fish not only in the waters around the islands but also along the coastline of the Qatar peninsula.

The osprey is a bird of prey with a highly-specialized diet, living almost exclusively on fish. However, the ospreys nesting on the Huwar Islands are known to include Socotra cormorants as a regular part of their diet. Although it closely resembles other fish-eating birds of prey such as eagles, the osprey is a unique species. It belongs to a family of its own, the genus *Pandion* and the species *haliaetus*, the latter meaning 'sea-eagle' in Greek. There are four subspecies in the world, the nominate *haliaetus* breeds in Europe, North Africa and the Middle East. The three other sub-species, which vary slightly in size and colouring, breed in North America, the Caribbean and Australasia.

An adult bird is around 60cm in length, with a wingspan of between 145 and 165 cm. The upper parts are dark brown but the flanks and belly are white with a brown band across the breast, so that it is sometimes mistaken for a large gull as it swoops and glides. The head is white, with a distinctive dark brown stripe through the brilliant yellow eye, reaching to the back of the neck. The powerful legs are greenish-grey and equipped with long black talons, with a reversible outer toe, allowing the osprey to grip fish with two talons forward and two back, the rough scaly skin on the feet providing further purchase. It catches fish by plunging onto its prey and snatching the fish from the water in its talons. Once in the air, the bird manoeuvres its catch so that the body of the fish is aligned with the direction of flight, to provide minimum wind resistance. The powerful black beak is strongly hooked for tearing up its meal. Ospreys can be distinguished from true fishing eagles by their long, narrow wings which are distinctively angled while gliding.

In Qatar, ospreys are both resident and migrant. Elsewhere they usually build their large, untidy nests of sticks at the top of tall trees, but here, where suitable trees are not available, they have no choice but to nest on the ground, choosing jebel outcrops or small, rocky islands. Usually between two and four eggs are laid, but it is rare for all the chicks to survive - one or two is the norm.

Ospreys may well have nested on the mainland of Qatar in the past, but owing to the increased human population they have moved out to the islands around the coast. Many visitors to Khor Al Adaid (the Inland Sea) have seen the huge nest towering atop a rocky pillar between two islets on the far side of the lagoon, with a spectacular background of barren hills of pink-coloured rock. It offers a

Left: Osprey nest on headland, the Huwar Islands
Right: Osprey with catch

golden opportunity for bird watchers to observe the comings and goings of the resident ospreys without disturbing them. We have been watching ospreys at this nest annually for over two decades, and have often seen the adult male soaring high and then repeatedly swooping over the sea, the pale underside of his wings gleaming, while his mate watches from the nest. From time to time he makes his display call, a distinctive high-pitched 'kee-kee-kee-kee'. In some years immature juveniles from the previous year's hatching will return and occupy the nest without breeding. Another nest about 1,500m away stands on a small, low-lying island in the inner lagoon.

It is surprising that ospreys in that barren environment are able to collect sufficient material to build such a huge nest. The nest itself is many years old, but each breeding pair refurbishes and rearranges it before settling down to egg-laying and incubation. We have seen ospreys flying towards it carrying what appeared to be branches in their talons. In that treeless land they must have covered long distances to collect them. They also make use of dried sea-weed, and sometimes human debris such as driftwood, and lengths of polypropylene rope. The nest is lined with seaweed and seagrass, and the construction of such huge nests represents a substantial amount of time and energy.

Osprey chick
in nest

As mentioned earlier, ospreys are remarkably tolerant of the presence of man. In Europe they have been known to construct their nests on electricity pylons and coastal navigation beacons. In North America they are even encouraged to build their nests close to human habitation so that people can enjoy watching their movements. In Qatar in the early spring of 1993, an osprey used a flagpole in the back garden of the Embassy of Japan in the West Bay area of Doha as a perching post for his morning's fishing activities. Only metres away from the windows of the building, he was to be seen each day for several weeks, turning his head this way and that to survey the sea, then launching himself into the air to return to the pole with a fish struggling in his talons.

It is estimated that there are currently around 30,000 breeding pairs of ospreys in the world. So at present the species is not endangered, but this was not always the case. Not so long ago they were ruthlessly hunted in Europe, along with all other birds of prey, and their eggs were either bought by collectors or smashed by vandals. Although this still happens (nests in Scotland are regularly raided, and some have to be given a 24-hour guard), laws carrying harsh penalties have been passed in many European countries to protect the osprey and these help to deter almost all but the most determined criminals. The fate of ospreys in Europe is closely linked, of course, with that of our own resident birds, as they are a migratory species.

The history of ospreys in Britain has been well-documented and makes sad reading. In the Middle Ages the species would have been distributed throughout the British Isles, nesting by rivers and lakes as well as on sea coasts. Relentless persecution throughout the 18th and 19th centuries drove the bird into its last retreat, the mountainous wilds of Scotland. The last pair nested in Ireland in 1800 and in England in 1842. It managed to hang on in Scotland until 1916, when the last pair nested in Inverness-shire. It was then extinct as a breeding species until its return in 1954 as a direct result of increased protection in Scandinavia.

Today, thanks to the setting up of reserves and the thousands of hours spent by volunteers guarding the nests against the depredations of collectors, there are enough breeding pairs in Scotland to ensure its continuation there, but it has still not been reintroduced to other areas of Britain. Much has been done to educate the public and thousands of people every year enjoy watching breeding ospreys from specially constructed hides. The same is true of many other European countries and of North America.

In Europe people travel long distances for the pleasure of watching ospreys at the reserves, and pay for the privilege, so in Qatar we are fortunate in being able to freely observe these magnificent birds both nesting and fishing. When the Qatar Natural History Group was established in 1978 it adopted the osprey as its logo, a fitting representative of the beautiful and varied wild life of this region.

Inland sea at dusk

SEA TURTLES

IN THE GOLDEN LIGHT OF A LATE AFTERNOON IN MAY, A TURTLE LAY QUIETLY RESTING in the shallow waters that surrounded a small, remote island, waiting for nightfall. Her mottled shell with its shades of amber, green and brown blended perfectly with the surrounding coral and anenomes, while the network of rippled light cast by the sun on the surface of the sea three metres above lent further camouflage. Only her head moved, as she turned a dark eye on a pair of divers who lay on the sandy sea-bed observing her Still, she made no move to swim away, her mind occupied with the task ahead. When darkness came she would leave the water for the beach, dig a deep hole and deposit around 150 soft-shelled, round white eggs the size of ping-pong balls, before covering them and returning swiftly to the safety of the sea.

The island was Sharoua, off the eastern coastline of Qatar. The turtle we were watching, in the summer of 1996, was a Hawksbill. Of the seven varieties of turtle found in the tropical seas of the world, four occur in Qatari waters. They are the Green turtle (*Chelonia mydas*), the Hawksbill (*Eretmochelys imbricate*), the Leatherback (*Dermochelys coriacea*) and the Olive Ridley (*Lepidochelys olivacea*). Of these, only the Hawksbill has breeding grounds in Qatar.

Worldwide, these gentle, harmless inhabitants of the sea are under threat, with some species faced with possible extinction. Turtles have roamed the oceans of the world for around 200,000,000 years, but in the

Top: Hawksbill turtle
Middle: Turtles mating
Bottom: Loggerhead turtle
Left: Abandoned fishing gear is a hazard for turtle hatchlings

last few decades their numbers have plummeted. For centuries turtles have been hunted for their meat, oil and shells, but now they fall victim to the curses of the modern age: poisoned by pollution, drowned by fishing lines and monofilament nets, mangled by speed-boat propellers, their nest sites disturbed by the building of high-rise hotels and the development of holiday resorts. In 1993 the Gulf Times published a detailed report about the threat to the turtles in Qatari waters which contained photographs of turtles openly displayed for sale at the Salwa Road fish market, along with turtle eggs.

A law had been passed in 1985 by the government of Qatar prohibiting 'the gathering and catching of sea birds' eggs and turtles', but the ruling was being ignored and it was not actively enforced. After more publicity in both the Arabic and the English press, turtles stopped appearing on open sale. The law was re-drafted in 2002, with penalties of fines or imprisonment for those who infringe it.

In 1996 the Environment Protection Committee, now incorporated into the Supreme Council for the Environment and Natural Reserves (SCENR), carried out an investigation into the habitats of sea birds and turtles around the coast. Their report, published in June that year, made depressing reading. Turtle nests were being robbed with impunity on the northern offshore sandspits of Umm Tais and Ras Reccan, and on mainland beaches like Fuwairat. It seemed that, despite constant publicity in newspapers and on television about protecting endangered species, some people were either ignorant of the law or indifferent to it.

Turtle Researchers at Fuwairit 2005 Left: a turtle is tagged Right: a turtle is weighed

Even without the problems caused by humans, a turtle's chances of surviving to adulthood are very small. Eggs are destroyed by fungi or fly larvae while still in the ground, and predators like foxes take the eggs before they hatch. The most dangerous moment for a turtle hatchling is the frantic sprint between nest site and sea. Birds, crabs and mammals wait to feast on the defenceless young, and once in the sea many more are eaten by fish. Man has now reduced their natural survival chance from one in a hundred to a ratio of far, far less.

Until recently remarkably little was known about turtles and their unique way of life. Serious research on turtles only began in 1954 in the United States, when biologists commenced investigations in Costa Rica to find out why Green turtle populations in the Caribbean were declining. Each species of turtle has its own specialized niche in the environment. Some eat crustaceans, others eat jellyfish and others prefer sea grass or sponges.

Female turtles always return to lay their eggs on or near the beach where they themselves hatched. Males may never return to land again once they hatch, nearing shore only to mate. They travel thousands of miles in migratory patterns that are still not fully understood.

After mating, the female turtle takes two to four weeks to emerge onto the beach and lay the first clutch of eggs. A mated turtle carries up to 800 eggs, which develop in batches of between 100 and 200 at a time. Thus, the female is carrying eggs in various stages of development. After laying her first clutch of eggs, she will wait two weeks until the next batch is ready. In the Arabian Gulf turtles usually lay about three clutches. But despite the enormous number of eggs laid by each female, the survival rate of hatchlings has been calculated at < 0.01.

Hawksbill turtles dig their nests on sandy beaches, hollowing out an egg-chamber. The sand has to be well-ventilated for the eggs to develop, as gases are excreted during the period of incubation. Sand that is too fine or too coarse is unsuitable, which may be the reason why in Qatar turtles nest only north of Al Khor and on some of the offshore islands.

The most common, relatively speaking, of the turtles in local waters is the Green turtle, which feeds on shallow sea grass pastures and so is more likely to be seen in coastal waters. In the past I have occasionally spotted them from the Doha Corniche, but I have not heard of any sightings as close to Doha in recent years. Green turtles can reach a shell length of 1.2m and weigh up to 200 kilos. The shell is dark green, with darker markings giving a mottled effect. Unlike the shell of the Hawksbill turtle, the scutes, or plates, on the Green turtle's carapace do not overlap.

Perhaps because it is a herbivore, the meat of the Green turtle was, and still is in some countries, the most valued of any. The fat used to be boiled with the cartilage to make a tasty soup and was much prized in 19th century Europe as a gourmet delicacy.

The Hawksbill turtle is smaller and less common in Qatari waters than the Green. A slow grower, its shell when adult is around 90 cms in length and its weight between 50 and 100 kilos. Hawksbills can live as long as 100 years, reaching sexual maturity at 30. The shell is an amber colour, with markings shading through black and brown to red and dark yellow. It is a reef dweller, often inhabiting a reef near its nesting site, and its preferred food is the sponges which grow on the reefs. It is unique among the turtle species in that it does not migrate long distances between its feeding and nesting grounds.

Unlike Green turtles, which are slow movers on land, Hawksbills leave the water very fast to lay their eggs and scurry back to the safety of the sea once the job is completed. They can raise themselves on their flippers to increase their speed.

Because of its beautiful mottled markings, the shell of the Hawksbill was used to make ornamental combs, spectacle frames and other small items. Japan was the chief importer of turtle shell for this industry. Until 1992, when the trade was finally stopped under pressure from the United States, Japan had been importing up to 31,000 shells each year.

Leatherbacks, which are occasionally seen far out in the waters of the Gulf by people in boats or aircraft, are giants among turtles. The largest ever recorded weighed almost 1000 kilos and measured 3 metres in length. The average weight of a leatherback is probably around 400 kilos. Unlike other turtles, Leatherbacks do not have hard plates but a soft skin covering their shell, on which are seven prominent ridges running the length of the shell. They very rarely come close to shore except to breed, preferring the open ocean, where they feed on jellyfish and plankton. Leatherbacks have been recorded diving to depths of 475 metres and can tolerate cold better than other turtles, as they have a thick, oil-saturated layer beneath their skin.

In contrast to the gigantic Leatherback is the little Olive Ridley, smallest of all marine turtles and sometimes seen feeding in Qatari waters. World-wide it is probably the

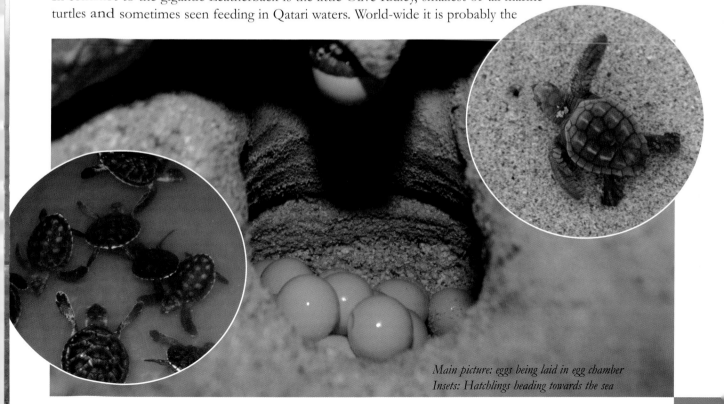

Main picture: eggs being laid in egg chamber
Insets: Hatchlings heading towards the sea

DUGONGS - GENTLE DENIZENS OF THE OCEAN

UNTIL THE LAST CENTURY THE ARABIAN GULF HAD A LARGE POPULATION OF DUGONGS. They provided a valuable source of protein for the people who for centuries fished and hunted around the shores of the Gulf. On the island of Umm an Nar, just off Abu Dhabi City, dugong bones and tusks were found in the remains of a village and in tombs dating from 2,700 BC. So numerous were the animals that the few taken by humans for food would have made no difference at all to the population.

It is estimated that the maximum sustainable annual harvest of marine mammals is 2% of the total population. Even as late as the 1970s dugong were still widely being caught and eaten by local people; their skin being turned into leather and their fat rendered down into oil. By daily visits to the fish *souq* in Abu Dhabi in the late seventies, one researcher estimated that the annual catch delivered was between 50 and 70 animals. Today, it is a different story. The countries of the region are struggling to keep this species safe from extinction. A slow moving, gentle marine mammal, it is an easy animal to kill and the numbers of dugong

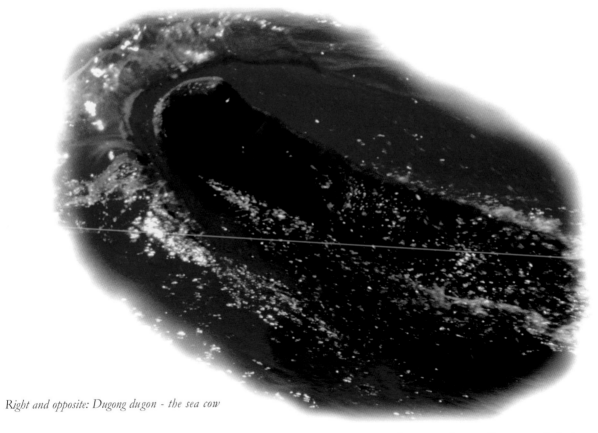

Right and opposite: Dugong dugon - the sea cow

(*Dugong dugon*) in the Arabian Gulf have dwindled, largely due to the influence of man. Because of their very slow rate of reproduction, they cannot sustain heavy culling.

Slaughtered for centuries for its meat, hide and bones, entangled and drowned in fishing nets, poisoned by oil spills, and starved as a result of the dredging of the seagrass beds on which it depends for survival, the dugong is now listed as an endangered species and is protected under several international treaties. Dugongs are no longer hunted, but many still die from being hit by boat propellers or being caught in monofilament fishing nets. Poisoning from heavy metals and polychlorinated biphenyls (PCBs) is also a hazard, and noise pollution from shipping and offshore development disturbs the animals.

Although a marine mammal, the dugong is more closely related to elephants and hyraxes than to whales or

MARINE MAMMALS

MAKING A SPLASH IN QATARI WATERS

NO ONE EVER FORGETS THEIR FIRST SIGHTING OF A DOLPHIN. THERE IS SOMETHING about the seemingly joyous way in which they speed through the water, leaping and criss-crossing the bow-wave of boats, their mouths curved in a friendly 'grin', that makes them instantly appealing. Their apparent benevolence towards humans is legendary. Everyone knows the tales, dating back to ancient Roman times, of dolphins supporting drowning swimmers. Ancient Arab seafarers believed that they brought good fortune to travellers. Their images occur worldwide, on ancient Greek pottery, in sculptures, on Roman mosaic pavements and even on coins. The word dolphin comes from the classical Greek *delphis,* meaning 'womb', because for the Greeks the dolphin symbolized birth and renewal of life.

In antiquity, just as now, there were numerous stories of dolphins allowing people to ride on their backs. Yet not many people know much about dolphins themselves, and scientists say that there is much yet to be discovered. In many ways, their lives are a mystery.

Dolphins, porpoises and whales belong to the order of mammals known as cetaceans. The distinction between whales and dolphins is less clearly defined than that between dolphins and porpoises: the so-called Killer Whale, or *Orca,* is in fact the largest species of dolphin. Porpoises are smaller than dolphins, with a stockier body. They have a low, or sometimes no, dorsal fin and have no 'beak', whereas on most species of dolphin the 'beak' is easily identified. The family of porpoises (*Phocoenidae*), is a small one, numbering only about six species worldwide. All porpoises have uniquely-shaped spatulate teeth, quite distinct from the sharply-pointed teeth of dolphins.

Here in Qatari waters we are fortunate in having several species of dolphins and one species of porpoise, plus, possibly, three species of baleen whales. Anyone can see dolphins here, with a bit of luck, and you don't even need to venture out to sea. We have observed them in the bay near the Gulf Sheraton Hotel, and from the beaches of Messai'eed and Fuwairit on the east coast, Ras Abrouq in the west, and of course, at Khor al Adaid, the Inland Sea. Once when we camped there a pod of dolphins came into the shallows beside the beach to investigate the kerosene lamp we had hung on a pole, and woke us with their snorting and blowing.

Sports divers use boats at the weekends to visit and dive on offshore wrecks, and schools of dolphins are frequently observed.

On one occasion a school of thirteen Long-beaked Common Dolphins surrounded the boat while it was anchored on a wreck. Divers were scrambling into their gear to get into the water and join them, when suddenly it was noticed that the creatures circling the boat were actually eleven dolphins and two large Tiger Sharks! This is not the first time that sharks have been observed to accompany dolphins.

Above: Dolphins at play   Opposite page: Orca or killer whale

Among the dolphins recorded in the waters of Qatar are the universally-familiar Common Bottlenose Dolphin (*Tursiops truncatus*) - the one with the pronounced beak and familiar 'grin' – and its slightly smaller relative the Indian Ocean Bottlenose Dolphin (*Tursiops aduncus*). The Indo-Pacific Humpback Dolphin (*Sousa chinensis*) is also seen here. Both *Tursiops* and *Sousa* are generally to be found in inshore waters. *Tursiops* has a shorter, more snubbed beak than *Sousa*, and generally swims much faster. The bodies of both are dark grey above and lighter beneath.

Further out to sea you are more likely to encounter the Long-beaked Common Dolphin (*Delphinus capensis*). Found throughout the oceans of the world, it is easy to identify with its slender, streamlined silhouette and long beak. The back is black or dark grey, with a white belly, and there is a distinctive hourglass-shaped pattern of grey and cream on the flanks. In Qatar Long-beaked Common Dolphins travel in larger groups than Bottlenose Dolphins; but they do not reach the really massive group sizes of this species in the Gulf of Oman and Arabian Sea, where thousands of individuals have been seen travelling together. This dolphin enthusiastically rides the bow-waves of ships, and is capable of spectacular leaps, sometimes clearing the surface of the sea by three or four metres. Long-beaked Common Dolphins are so named to distinguish them

Bottle-nosed dolphins

from the Short-beaked Common Dolphins (*Delphinus delphis*). The distinction between the two species was recognized only quite recently.

Pantropical Spotted Dolphins (*Stenella attenuata*) have also been recorded in Qatari waters. Researchers can estimate the age of an individual dolphin by the distribution of spots on the body. It is also possible that the Spinner Dolphin (*Stenella longirostris*) occurs locally, as it has been observed elsewhere in the Arabian Gulf.

In July 1994 a group of sports divers reported seeing 'a pair of small, light grey dolphins with no dorsal fins'

Humpback dolphin

which crossed the bow of their boat at speed as they were heading towards Doha. In fact, what they were probably fortunate enough to have seen was a pair of Finless Porpoises (*Neophocaena phocaenoides*). They often travel in pairs and are the only porpoise without a dorsal fin. The populations of Finless Porpoises have been badly affected by pollution in other parts of Asia and this is possibly the only recorded sighting in Qatari waters.

No one knows for sure why some species can manage with a small dorsal fin or even no fin at all, while in others the fin can be as tall as 180 cm, as it is in the Orca. It may help with balance, or it may have a signalling function assisting various species to recognise each other quickly.

Commercial divers here have reported dolphins coming to watch them at work, apparently fascinated by human activity. A favourite story is of a pair of dolphins which arrived daily to keep pairs of divers company as they worked on a pipeline at Messai'eed. The dolphins deliberately imitated the clumsy swimming movements of the divers, waggling their bodies up and down and making eye contact as if inviting their human 'friends' to share the joke. As each pair of divers surfaced after 30 minutes the dolphins raced back to the beginning of the pipeline, ready to join the next pair as they descended. This continued for weeks until the work was completed.

A group of sports divers on one of the two artificial reefs at Messai'eed were joined by several dolphins who caught fish in their mouths and then deliberately brought them to show the divers before swallowing them, seeming to indicate, 'Look what I can do!' It is no wonder that humans have long felt an affinity with dolphins.

One December morning a few years ago a party of divers camping near the mouth of Khor al Adaid, the Inland Sea, observed three large whales approaching the shore. There were two adults and a calf which swam close to its mother. They swam parallel with the shore about 50m out, repeatedly surfacing and clearly curious about the on-shore watchers. These were Bryde's Whales (*Balaenoptera edeni*), which reach a maximum length of 14m. Two other baleen whales found in the Arabian Gulf are the Blue Whale (*Balaenoptera musculus*) and the Humpback Whale (*Megaptera novaeangliae*). In 2001 a dead Humpback Whale was washed up on a beach between Doha and Al Wakra. It is possible that the Bryde's Whale may live all year round in the Arabian Gulf and breed here. If so, they may be genetically isolated from other populations of this species of whale.

Chalcides ocellatus - the Garden Skink

Boxtree

ROLLING STONES
IMAGES OF THE WORLD TOUR 1989 - 1990

ROLLING STONES
IMAGES OF THE WORLD TOUR 1989 - 1990
Text by David Fricke and Robert Sandall
Additional text by Rod Green

First Published in the UK 1990
by BOXTREE LIMITED, 36 Tavistock Street, London WC2E 7PB

Copyright: ©1990 Musidor B.V.

Europe section of text © Robert Sandall 1990

USA section of text © David Fricke 1990

Other text © Boxtree Ltd. 1990

All Rights reserved

ISBN 1 8 5283 081 6

12345678910

Art and design direction: Mick Jagger, Charlie Watts, Lance Yates

Compiled by Tony King, Jane Rose, Lance Yates

Design by: Dave Crook

Editor: Rod Green

Photographers: Eugene Adebari, Mikio Agriga, George Chin, Claude Gassian,
Kevin Mazur, Paul Natkin, Dimo Safari, Albert Watson

Front Cover Photograph: Albert Watson

Printed in England by Clays Ltd., St. Ives plc

A CIP catalogue record for this book is available from the British Library

INTRODUCTION

They were alive, but were they kicking? Today, with the benefit of 15 months worth of hindsight and 115 packed out stadium shows in North America, Europe and Japan as hard evidence, the question sounds merely facetious. Back in early 1989, however, the outcome of what soon turned into the biggest, best attended and quite simply the best rock and roll tour ever, looked a lot less certain. The Stones hadn't ventured out on the road for 7 years, the longest such gap in their entire career. In the interim there had been births, marriages and solo careers to preoccupy individual band members, as well as one tragic death which, far more even than all the mischievous rumourmongering of the world's gutter press, had seriously threatened band unity for the first time. On December 12, 1985, the "sixth Stone", Ian Stewart, died of a heart attack. With his abrupt departure the group lost a founder member, a great piano player and a close friend whose comparative immunity to all the alienating rigmaroles of stardom had helped to keep everybody's mind on the job. Without "Stu", the famous five's unique cohesiveness was suddenly put at risk. And, what with one thing and another, by the time plans for Steel Wheels ground into motion 3 years later, the Stones weren't just winding up for another album with triumphal tour attached. In the public perception at least, they were attempting the most difficult move in the game. The Rolling Stones were making a comeback.

That they pulled it off so confidently was, in the event, only partly down to the enduring potency of the myth of "the greatest rock and roll band in the world". Sure, we all re-discovered the truth that some of those songs just will not grow old. Sure, the Stones proved yet again that they could pull in as many youthful "first timers" as they could returning regulars. But what held them there, in record numbers (over 6 million) this time, had a lot to do with the band's unprecedented attention to the fine detail of their performance on the one hand, and to a clear sighted vision of how to stage a show in a stadium on the other. The Stones managed to look enormous without sounding pompous or monumental. They were impressive and expressive at the same time. Here was a massively entertaining, grand spectacle which never neglected the intimacies and intricacies of the music that kick started everything in the first place. The person who came up with that line, "Think global, act local" must have been waiting for this tour to come to town.

Now, though, there is another question: will they, or when will they, be back? Nobody, of course, is saying anything very definite on this point. Jagger and Richards will point out that they have continuing solo interests; on the domestic front, wives and families claim more of everybody's attention these days. And you simply can't make a regular habit of leaving home and living out of suitcases for as long as this adventure lasted when time isn't quite on your side the way it used to be. But the smart money says that the Stones will hit the road again at some point, and for two very simple reasons. They still love what they do, and they are still very, very good at it.

Never been better, in fact.

Robert Sandall

MONTSERRAT

There were no guarantees when it all started. Having stowed their emotional baggage about the long-term future of the Rolling Stones (and their own personal relationship) in a dark corner somewhere, Mick Jagger and Keith Richards agreed to have another go at songwriting together in January, 1989. "I just ignored all that crap," Jagger said later, dismissing the battle of wills and wits which had escalated in the years after *Dirty Work*. "I thought we should just get on with it. You know, English people are like that. They carry on. Stiff upper lip."

For the next two months, at Eddy Grant's studio on the Caribbean island of Barbados, Jagger and Richards applied that stoical resolve to the job at hand with spectacular results. By quitting time in late February, there were 12 new songs bearing the Jagger/Richards brand, not to mention 40 or so leftovers - mostly unfinished melodies, riffs and lyrics - on the cutting room floor.

The productivity rate alone was impressive, but there was also a kick and class to the new material that had been lacking in recent Stones albums. On records like *Emotional Rescue* and *Tattoo You*, Jagger and Richards mostly fashioned new tunes from old, tarted-up outtakes or skeletal jam ideas. This time they started from scratch, realigning the intuitive creative balance that yielded some of their greatest triumphs - *Beggars Banquet, Let It Bleed, Sticky Fingers, Exile On Main Street*. They came up trumps.

The future singles *Mixed Emotions* and *Rock And A Hard Place* bristled with the refined primitivism of the band's best early seventies work. The bittersweet ache of *Almost Hear You Sigh* and *Slipping Away* showed that Jagger and Richards had not lost their ballad touch. For *Continental Drift* they even detoured back to the eastern modal investigations of *Paint It Black*.

Their enthusiasm proved contagious. When the full band convened at George Martin's AIR Studios in Montserrat to commence work on *Steel Wheels*, they played like they were training for a championship fight, cutting tracks and jamming for up to fifteen hours at a stretch. At one point in the sessions, Bill Wyman took a trip to nearby Antigua to fend off British tabloid snoops sniffing around for news on his impending wedding to Mandy Smith. While he was off hosting a press conference, the other Stones cranked out four tunes with Ron Wood on bass.

With Chris Kimsey (a veteran of Stones sessions since 1971) co-producing, the band cut the basic tracks for the album in only five weeks, recording everything live in the studio.

"This music, it's certainly not Beethoven or Mozart," Richards said with evident delight during the mixing sessions later in London. "It's got nothing to do with intricacy. It's got to do with a bunch of guys making accidents together, spontaneity and an immediate form of communication."

Just like old times.

Sheik Jagger jams with the Master Musicians of Jajouka.

MOROCCO

The flight from London took only a couple of hours, but the time change was something else again. In mid-June, Mick Jagger and Keith Richards set off for a weekend of recording and serious *deja vu* in Morocco, where they had vacationed in the late sixties and where the late Brian Jones, had discovered the mystical 4000-year-old sounds of the Master Musicians of Jajouka. As the Tangier sun poured into a 16th century palace courtyard inside the historic Kasbah, Jagger (dressed like the Sheik of Shake in an elegant white kaftan) and Richards - joined by Ron Wood, who dashed in for the weekend as well - let the tapes roll and basked in the primal glow of the Master Musicians' joyous, untamed noise, the influence of which was eventually felt in *Continental Drift*.

CONNECTICUT

They didn't even say hello. They didn't have to. The staccato bark of Keith Richards' guitar at the beginning of *Start Me Up* said it all as the Stones launched their fall Steel Wheels sortie with an unannounced barroom warmup on August 12th at Toad's Place. In this 700–capacity club in New Haven, Connecticut, the Stones blitzed a packed house of delirious and very surprised fans with a searing fifty–minute set that augured well for the stadium spectaculars to come.

It was an evening of sweat, smiles and swinging from the rafters, of relishing the sexual thrust and banshee scream of rock & roll in its native garage and barroom environment. Unsuspecting fans had paid a paltry $3.01 to get in, expecting just another Saturday night dance party. The opening act, a local combo called Sons of Bob, didn't realise they were *hors d'oeuvres* for the Stones until the band's gear arrived.

Secret pre–tour club shows were nothing new to the Stones; the '81 U.S. tour was prefaced by a riotous gig – with the emphasis on 'riot' – at a club in Worcester, Massachusetts which was beseiged by angry fans who couldn't get in. At Toad's Place, though, the fireworks were all indoors as the Stones, assisted by Leavell and Clifford at the ivories, ripped through *Miss You, It's Only Rock 'n' roll* and *Brown Sugar* with vintage verve. *Sad, Sad, Sad,* and *Mixed Emotions* from the as yet unreleased *Steel Wheels* made their stage debuts and halfway through the set the band dropped down into a lean, mean version of Willie Dixon's *Little Red Rooster* – a relic from their purist R&B days – that would later be a highlight of the outdoor shows.

The Toad's Place rave–up was a kind of Graduation Day party for the Stones, marking the end of a seven–week residency in suburban Connecticut packed solid with intensive rehearsals, tour production meetings and promotional activities for the new album. It had already been a work intensive year for the band. Steel Wheels was written, recorded and mixed in a dizzying six months – record time for a band that, in recent, years, had regularly taken thrice that to make an album. Yet within a week of tidying up the final mixes at Olympic Studios in London, the Stones and their entourage had set up camp in the rural hamlet of Washington, Connecticut. The local population swelled overnight with the band's families, friends, business

A ghetto blaster gave the press a taste of *Mixed Emotions.*
The *Mixed Emotions* video was recorded during rehearsals in Connecticut. (left and opposite right)

associates and tour personnel while the Stones commandeered Wykeham Rise, a former girls' boarding school, as a practise space.

And practise they did. "We just shut the door and played," recalled ex–Allman Brothers pianist Chuck Leavell, who divided up keyboard duties with young British sessioneer Matt Clifford. The Stones' original "wish" list for the show ran to 75 songs – which would have made the show about six hours long. That was eventually pared down by more than half, to a more manageable 28 songs, with a few numbers popping in and out of the set as the tour progressed. *Play With Fire* was replaced in the ballad spot by *Angie* in mid–route; *Shattered* was dropped after the first night in Philadelphia; *Salt Of The Earth*, a rarely aired gem from *Beggar's Banquet*, would be dusted off for the big end–of–tour blow out in Atlantic City.

On July 11th, the Stones took the day off for a trip to New York City, where they played host to the world's press with characteristic flamboyance. After letting 450 international newshounds bake in near–hundred degrees heat for about an hour in an

American choreographer Lavelle Smith puts Mick through his paces.

un–air–conditioned waiting room at Grand Central Station, the band pulled into track 42 aboard a chartered commuter train, riding in a Roaring Twenties–style caboose which had been featured in Francis Ford Coppola's film, *The Cotton Club*. Jagger made a short, perfunctory speech about the *Steel Wheels* tour and album, gave the press a tantalizing taste of *Mixed Emotions* on a little boom box and, with Richards, verbally deflected the generally hapless questions with practiced *hauteur*.

Q: "Some rock critics have charged that the only reason you're doing it is for the money."

Jagger: "What about love and fame and fortune? Have you forgotten about all those things?"

To which Keith Richards added with impish glee, "The glory, darlin', the glory!"

With Connecticut reeling in their wake, the Stones decamped for Long Island where they set up shop at Nassau Coliseum for dress rehearsals with the complete "industrial holocaust" stage set and full lights 'n' pyro. In less than three weeks it would be opening night and the feast of glory would begin.

START ME UP

After seven years off the road, the Rolling Stones weren't about to just walk on stage each night and say "Hi, (your city here), did you miss us?" As it was on the '81-'82 tour, *Start Me Up* - an *Emotional Rescue* outtake later hammered into shape for *Tattoo You* - was the opening salvo. This time around, though, the Stones transformed the song into a declaration of war, prefacing the metallic cackle of Keith Richards' opening riff with a nuclear chorus of fireworks and a wall of fire three hundred feet across. When the smoke cleared, Richards had dropped down into his fighting crouch, choking the neck of his Telecaster with undisguised vigour. Ron Wood, cigarette dangling precipitously from his pursed lips, sprayed the crowd with bluesy shards of steely guitar. And Mick Jagger - no doubt piqued by charges that he veered dangerously close to self-parody on the last tour - was in firm command of centre stage, eschewing excessive sexual camp for the leonine cool of a veteran road warrior. With the Watts 'n' Wyman backfield maintaining rhythm order with their usual aplomb, it was more than enough, as the song goes, to make a grown man, or woman, cry - for joy.

STEEL WHEELS

The Rolling Stones had just whipped nearly 55,000 people at Veterans Stadium in Philadelphia into a roaring frenzy with a double welcoming whammy of *Start Me Up* and *Bitch*, and were mid-way through a steaming *Shattered* when the sound system - all 550,000 watts of it - went stone dead. After a year of planning, months of preparation and no expense spared, a single generator fault brought the Stones Steel Wheels juggernaut grinding to a brief, but nonetheless embarrassing, halt. On the opening night.

It took the engineers just three minutes to locate and rectify the problem - the only major bummer of the entire fourteen week North American tour. Knowing a bad omen when they saw it, the Stones dropped *Shattered* from the set list after the August 30th opening show and got down to the business of putting on the best single-act stadium show in the history of rock and roll.

The Stones, of course, invented the modern rock concert. Tightly choreographed package tours and breathless half-hour headline sets rendered inaudible by screaming teenage girls were still a fresh, rather unpleasant memory for the band

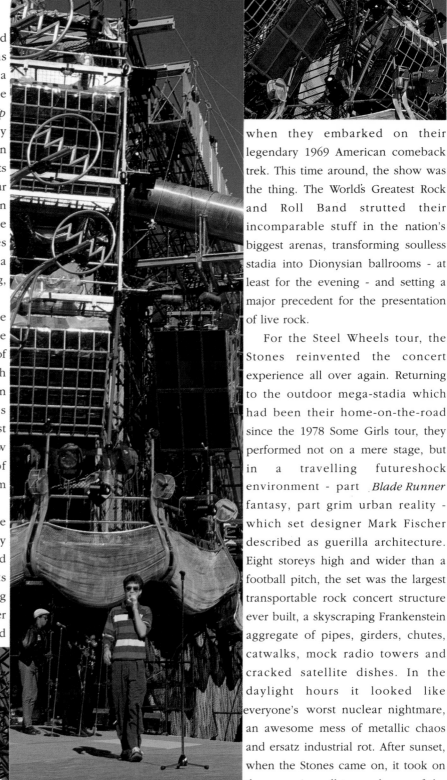

when they embarked on their legendary 1969 American comeback trek. This time around, the show was the thing. The World's Greatest Rock and Roll Band strutted their incomparable stuff in the nation's biggest arenas, transforming soulless stadia into Dionysian ballrooms - at least for the evening - and setting a major precedent for the presentation of live rock.

For the Steel Wheels tour, the Stones reinvented the concert experience all over again. Returning to the outdoor mega-stadia which had been their home-on-the-road since the 1978 Some Girls tour, they performed not on a mere stage, but in a travelling futureshock environment - part *Blade Runner* fantasy, part grim urban reality - which set designer Mark Fischer described as guerilla architecture. Eight storeys high and wider than a football pitch, the set was the largest transportable rock concert structure ever built, a skyscraping Frankenstein aggregate of pipes, girders, chutes, catwalks, mock radio towers and cracked satellite dishes. In the daylight hours it looked like everyone's worst nuclear nightmare, an awesome mess of metallic chaos and ersatz industrial rot. After sunset, when the Stones came on, it took on the menacing, all-too-real aura of the oil and chemical refineries belching

Guns 'N' roses supported the Stones in Los Angeles and the Gunners'lead singer, W. Axl Rose, flew into Atlantic City to join Mick on stage.

Award winning band Living Colour filled the regular support slot on the Steel Wheels tour. Living Colour's 1988 debut album, *Vivid*, sold over two million copies worldwide, paving the way for their follow–up, *Time's Up*. They were voted "Best New American Band" in the '89 Rolling Stone Readers' Poll.

deathsmoke along the New Jersey Turnpike.

The basic design arithmetic was apocalyptic itself. It took as many as 120 people around a week to erect the stages; that's right, there were two of them, leapfrogging from stadium to stadium. The radio towers rose so far above the scaffolding, topping off at 130 feet, that federal law required the installation of blinking red aircraft collision lights (which made the whole thing look even more authentic). The show's entire pyro package - including the big bang finale, accompanied by Bizet's *March of the Toreadors* - featured nearly 50,000 fireworks and 100,000 pounds of aerial shells, not to mention a ton of flash powder.

But instead of being dwarfed by the physical immensity of the stage and its dramatic air of rack and ruin, the Stones reigned over it all like kings of the slum, celebrating their own weather-beaten durability and indomitable spirit with hardened muscle and outlaw vigour. "It had to reflect the Rolling Stones story in 1989," lighting designer Patrick Woodroffe said of the Steel Wheels spectacle in one interview. "It had to have dignity. It had to be tough, hard and current rather than nostalgic and beautiful."

Like the music itself the Stones had everything to prove, and lose, by their nightly stage raids. After so long off the road and a less-than-lustrous mid-eighties studio streak, the Stones were competing not only with their spiritual offspring dogging them on the charts (Guns 'N' Roses et al.) but with their own daunting legacy.

Nothing less than their integrity and continuing relevance were at stake.

That they still like nothing better than a good kick up the caboose before going on was apparent in their choice of opening act, the killer black rock band Living Colour. Jagger had been instrumental in getting the group a record deal, producing two demos for them in '87, and he knew what they were capable of; raging psycho-funk, smouldering blues and hurricane thrash, all charged with the racial pride and soul-fire that had been the hallmark of the Stones' great opening acts through the years - Ike and Tina Turner, B. B. King, Stevie Wonder, The Meters, Prince.

For their four night run at the Memorial Coliseum in Los Angeles, the Stones even upped the ante by booking LA premier badasses Guns 'N' Roses as special guests. With all due respect to the Gunners, who certainly wowed their friends and neighbours, it was "like putting a Honda scooter on a highway with a Harley", as one critic put it in the Village Voice. The Stones had age, experience, tunes and undiminished insolence on their side. And they came by their attitude naturally - they were born with it.

Richards sounded reveille every night with the familiar

Tele stutter of *Start Me Up*, but it was Jagger - first appearing in white shirt , tight black pants and Napoleonesque green tails - who set the tone of the evening. He wailed with lusty strength and unmistakable commitment. The nervous agitation in his trademark sexual karate belied the practised grace and dynamic exaggeration with which he worked the stage and played to the cameras broadcasting his every manoeuvre on the giant video screens. He made the most of the latter especially during *2000 Light Years From Home*, when his slow-mo shadow dancing was set against a "vintage" sixties oil-bubble light show.

After so long it's easy to take the Stones' greatest strengths for granted - the slash and snarl of Keef and Woody's guitar crossfire, the bedrock rhythms of Bill Wyman and Charlie Watts, the harsh argumentative lyricism with which Jagger and Richards have documented the high costs and tainted rewards of bedroom politics and emotional warfare. But *One Hit (To The Body)*, a *Dirty Work* number new to the live repertoire, was a brilliantly rude awakening, riveting in its frank brutality. The taut, torrid version of *Gimme Shelter* - capping an epic suite featuring *Paint It Black, 2000 Light Years From Home* and *Sympathy For The Devil* - was shot through with Altamont horror and Crack City paranoia. Jagger's

rousing duet with backing singer Lisa Fischer, who sang like one of Hells Belles, was a chilling highlight of every show.

The North American leg of the Rolling Stones world tour came to a suitably impressive climax on December 20th with a radio and cable TV simulcast of the final show at the Atlantic City Convention Center, where the band played to a bizarre mix of hardcore fans and high rollers from the boardwalk casinos. Eric Clapton dropped by to turn up the blues heat on *Little Red Rooster* (as he had on other stops on the tour), W. Axl Rose and Izzy Stradlin of Guns 'N' Roses did their "junior glimmer twins" thing on a one-night-only performance of *Salt Of The Earth* and the Stones themselves paid tribute to their deep blues roots, bringing on John Lee Hooker to lead them through some feelgood boogie.

The Steel Wheels extravaganza was never about simply making rock history come alive. The Stones rammed that point home every night during *It's Only Rock And Roll*, leaning into the song like they'd just written it the day before, while a pantheon of rock immortals paraded across the video screens - Berry, Holly, Presley, Hendrix, Led Zeppelin and, of course, the spotty '64 Stones. Now, as then, the Stones were out to prove that this was history in the making - and they were far from finished.

HARLEM SHUFFLE

Number six in the evening's hit parade, sandwiched between *Undercover of the Night* and *Tumbling Dice*, the Stones' saucy reading of *Harlem Shuffle* was their loving nod to the gritty urban R&B of the early sixties which they had tried so hard to emulate in their formative years. First waxed by Bob and Earl in 1963, the original *Harlem Shuffle* was a robust dancefloor strut stoked with muscle. On stage - as they did in the studio when they cut the song for *Dirty Work* - the Stones revamped the song into a wonderfully sinuous,

boldly sexual romp, jacking up the guitar aggro while
Charlie Watts nailed down the beat with blithe precision.
Jagger worked the stage with a cocky flair that would have
gone down a storm on audition night at the Apollo Theatre,
making the most of the song's down-home lyric flourishes
("Do the monkey, chi-*yi-yi-yi*-ild!"). And when he hit that
big opening "Wooo!" at New York's Shea Stadium with
backup singers Bernard Fowler, Lisa Fischer and Cindy
Mizelle, you can bet they heard it all the way over on 125th.

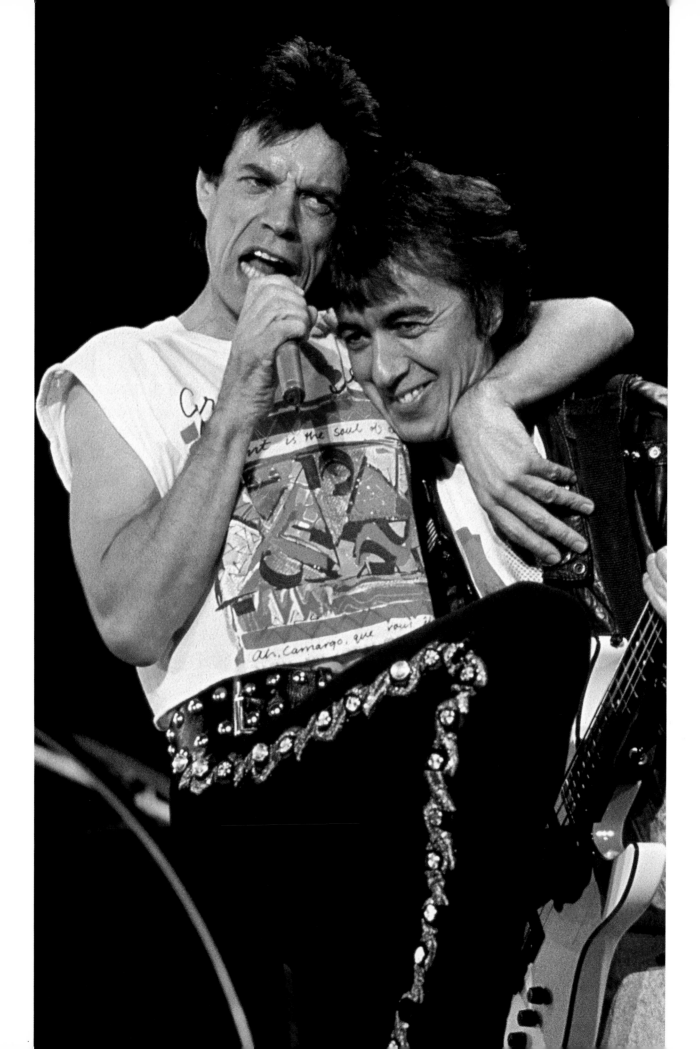

THE STAGE

The beginnings of an abstract thought, an elusive and ephemeral concept, can be a tricky customer to deal with. When Mick Jagger started to think about how the '89-'90 Stones tour would look, he knew that he was going to need help pinning down his ideas. What he wanted was the largest, most elaborate stage set ever constructed for a rock show - and this Herculean task eventually fell to Fisher Park Ltd.

The Stones knew Fisher Park's work from stages they had designed for other major shows, including Tina Turner, Janet Jackson and Pink Floyd's The Wall. Steel Wheels, however, had to be different. Architect Mark Fisher started to turn Jagger's ideas into a visual reality. Sketches and drawings were produced and amended; scale models were constructed and altered. Consulting constantly with Jagger and Charlie Watts, they gradually evolved the design concept, bringing in the lighting and sound designers, too, as Mark and his partner Jonathan Park began to get down to the nuts and bolts of the construction. Of course, it didn't take long to realise that Steel Wheels was too big to be lugged around Europe and, rather than simply scale down the original stage set, a whole new design was needed, retaining all the paradoxical imagery of urban vitality and industrial decay. Fisher presented the first Urban Jungle ideas to the Stones in New York in January 1990 and on Valentine's Day in Tokyo, Mark, Mick and Charlie pored over the final scale model of the show that was poised to take Europe by storm.

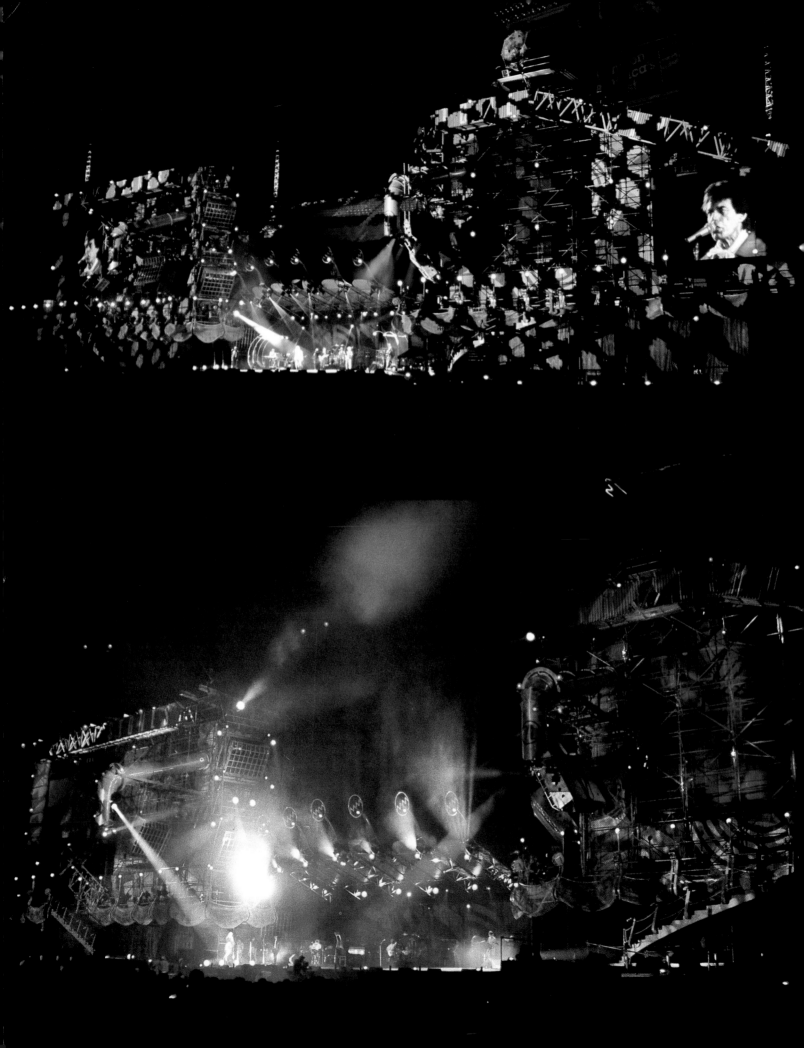

LIGHTS

There had been talk of a Rolling Stones tour. Patrick Woodroffe had worked with Mick Jagger on Jagger's solo tour and there had been talk of how the lighting might be handled should the Stones ever tour again.

A phone call from Barbados brought the flights of fancy into focus. Jagger and Richards were there, working together, planning a new album, planning a tour. It was to be the most spectacular rock show ever staged and it had to have the most spectacular illumination imaginable. Woodroffe was the man with the expertise and inspiration to bring it all together.

The lighting design evolved through a series of meetings, notably in Montserrat where the Stones gathered to begin recording, during which the concepts of the Steel Wheels and Urban Jungle stage designs were formulated.

Woodroffe's idea was to reflect the scale of the stage set, the scale of the venues the band would play and the scale of the events themselves with lighting on an equally fantastic scale. Rather than sprinkle the stage with thousands of smaller lights, Woodroffe settled for just eight colossal 50,000 watt units inspired by the stadium lights. Incorporated in each was a giant Megamac colour scrolling device developed for the tour by Light and Sound Design of Birmingham.

Gels leaked across the front of the lights facilitating an effective and speedy colour change. These massive lights bathed the stage in a selection of twelve colours and were complemented by 70 Varilites and 200 architectural bulkhead lights which helped create the set's image of industrial decay.

In fact, there was as much emphasis placed on lighting the set as there was on lighting the performance area. The entire spectacle was intended to have as much visual appeal from the far end of the stadium as it did from in front of the stage. Those at the back of the crowd had to

be able to respond to the mood of each number even if, from where they were standing, the performance area seemed little bigger than a postage stamp. The same philosophy was employed on both Steel Wheels and Urban Jungle, although the techniques differed.

The Steel Wheels set was dead in daylight. Part of its appeal lay in the way that the dormant structure started to light up and glow as soon as the house lights went down. The whole thing came to life when the Stones hit the stage.

Urban Jungle, on the other hand, had to work visually unaided in the early evening daylight of the European venues, hence the garishly bright colours on the enormous hanging scrims. Rather than having colour slowly becoming apparent in the lighting, the dynamism of the band carried the show until darkness descended and the lighting effects kicked in, adding a whole new dimension to the performance.

Once the philosophizing and the conceptualizing had been turned into tangible lighting hardware, lighting directors Dave Hill and Charlie Wilson took over to run the lighting boards during the shows. Stored on computer were "scenes" Woodroffe, his staff and the band had created together. The lighting boards were then "played" almost like musical instruments to recall the required effects at precisely the right moment. At the same time, the 35 follow spot operators (union hands in the US but truck drivers and roadies in Europe to avoid language difficulties) and pyro technicians positioned all over the rigging followed instructions relayed through headphones.

Although the lighting effects never changed fundamentally from show to show, there was always something new to be incorporated as the whole performance was fine-tuned, adding a more extravagant effect to highlight a guitar solo or pull together a chorus. If it was ever felt that something could be done better, suggestions from all quarters were taken on board.

The most spectacular rock show ever staged, after all, had to have the most spectacular illumination imaginable.

JAPAN

The dark glasses did little to disguise the figure in the blue jacket striding purposefully towards the VIP reception suite. A legend can't hide behind a set of shades.

By his side, shrouded against the February chill in a camel coat and a white scarf was his long-time friend and musical partner. Together they advanced on the massed ranks of photographers and the waiting army of fans.

Mick Jagger and Charlie Watts had arrived at Tokyo's Narita Airport.

The day before, Keith Richards and Ronnie Wood had experienced a similar reception. The Rolling Stones were assembling for their first ever tour of Japan.

Bill Wyman had been delayed and would follow on a few days later, missing out on the Steel Wheels press conference at the Tokyo Dome, the venue for all ten of the Stones' Japanese shows.

The four Rolling Stones who did appear on the low stage for the benefit of the Japanese journalists looked relaxed and rested, having enjoyed a six week break after their exhausting 36 city North American tour. Flanked by an imposing honour guard of Samurai warriors, they smiled good naturedly and fielded a barrage of questions fired at them from the floor. The build-up to the Rolling Stones' Japanese debut had begun.

The days before the first show saw Rolling Stones fever sweep through the city. Massive merchandise displays in Tokyo record stores only served to feed the fans' hunger for anything bearing the band's imprimatur. It was a degree of enthusiasm which, according to the store managers, had never before been seen - not even when Michael Jackson was in town.

The Stones themselves determined to enjoy their stay in Japan. They indulged in a spot of sightseeing and a fun fair at the stadium was closed for the afternoon while the band, their families and some of the tour staff sampled a few thrills and spills. Keith and Ronnie joined the audience at the Tokyo Dome (the shape of the roof earned the venue its nickname, The Big Egg) for Mike Tyson's World Title fight on February 11th, watching usurper Buster Douglas strip the champ of his title.

Tyson, however, wasn't the only one with a headache when the fight finished. As soon as it was all over, the stage crews moved in, ripping out the boxing ring to make way for the Steel Wheels stage. The Japanese riggers had little more than two days before the first show. Everything was waiting, primed and ready to be loaded in, but the stage had never been built in such a short time before.

The show went ahead on schedule, of course, but behind the scenes as the Stones exploded onto the stage, was sprawled a team of weary riggers. Having worked round the clock to complete the erection, many of them simply fell fast asleep, missing the very first Rolling Stones performance in Japan.

Audience reaction to the world's greatest rock and roll band generally varied from a wild enthusiasm to an ecstatic frenzy, but the Japanese audience was something entirely different. Mick had already experienced the phenomenon on his solo tour, but for the rest of the band it was a new sensation. Having come straight from their offices, many of those in the crowd wore sober business suits and carried briefcases. A wave of applause would accompany an appreciated guitar solo or instrumental break and a thunderous roar would follow each number . . . dying to

absolute silence for the start of the next.

Crowd control on leaving the stadium was also markedly different from the anarchic rush and crush at western shows. Each section of the audience waited for an announcement over the PA instructing them to leave, then filed out of the appropriate exits in an orderly fashion - possibly the world's most polite rock 'n' roll rebels.

The band was whisked out of the stadium even before the crowd began its regimented departure. Before The Big Egg was entireley empty they were back in the Hotel Okura in the heart of Tokyo.

Mid-way through the band's stint at The Big Egg, their record company threw a party for a particular celebration. Traditionally, the Japanese celebrate a major occasion, such as a wedding or moving into a new house, with a special

sake ceremony. The lid of a wooden cask of the finest sake is smashed open with a wooden mallet and the contents sampled in traditional square wooden cups. The band was presented with a sake cask wrapped in a hemp jacket bearing the legend "The Very Honourable Rolling Stones", which they duly broke open after being awarded a platinum disc for sales of the Steel Wheels CD.

By the time the last fans were trooping out of The Big Egg, over half a million people had seen the Rolling Stones play live in Tokyo and the band's long overdue Japanese inauguration had been declared a resounding success. The day after the last show on February 27th, the Stones and their families went their separate ways, flying home to prepare for a different show on a different continent.

URBAN JUNGLE

The show which finally arrived in Europe in May 1990 and spent the rest of the summer there was a significantly different affair from the mighty Steel Wheels which had trundled across America and Japan. In the first place, the stage set had been completely re-designed. Gone were all those images redolent of dark satanic mills – the chutes, the overhangs, the extruded metallic thingies and chainmail balustrades. The general air of post-industrial mayhem of Steel Wheels had all been replaced by a brighter, lighter and more summery looking structure which relied on swirls of colour rather than tons of armour.

The concept, however, was essentially the same. Steel Wheels had grown out of Jagger's desire to create an industrial urban landscape that "looked more like a forest". This time it was the forest that was starting to look more citified. Both designs took their cue from the slightly futuristic architectural junkheaps portrayed in films such as *Blade Runner* or *Brazil*. Urban Jungle was styled more on the model of a derelict plantation house, overrun by weird mutated foliage and other, even more obstreperous, new life forms.

It sounded like a great idea. Its more compact size solved many of the problems inevitably associated with touring the slow roads of the frontier and customs-clogged territories of Europe. Including site preparation, Urban Jungle could be staged in six days where Steel Wheels needed ten. It weighed less and moved faster. By virtue of being more intrinsically colourful, it was also better suited to the sorts of curfew restrictions which bedevil outdoor rock events in many European cities. Steel Wheels was designed to be seen fully lit and in total darkness: Urban Jungle – like the set the Stones built for their daytime shows in 1982 – would make better sense in the long twilight of a summer evening. And from the band's point of view it offered a refreshing change, a different playing environment from the one they had already strutted and scampered all over on 70 separate occasions.

Despite all its advantages, Urban Jungle proved difficult to get right. The jungly, beast-ridden paintings of an American artist, John Alexander (popular with Jagger and the rest of the Stones), provided a promising starting point. The colourful exotic plants were thought to be fine but all those mandrills, alligators and parrots didn't promote quite the right image. To give the set the raw edge which was required, the tour logo was created. A wild four legged thing with a headful of jagged teeth, the general feeling was that this creature might once have been a dog and it was duly christened Skippy. The deranged canine theme caught on. To compensate for the loss of so many of the 3D elements in the Steel Wheels set, it was suggested that a pack of giant inflatable "Street Fighting Dogs" be introduced to spring into life during the opening bars of *Street Fighting Man*.

The problems came late, almost too late – after the set had been agreed and painted, and only three days before the first show in Rotterdam.

That mutant psychedelic foliage which always looked so good on paper (it was heavily featured in a fold-out centrespread in the official tour programme, and indeed stayed there) simply didn't work when transferred onto fabric scrim. A new design based loosely on images of primitive cave-painting used in the video for the band's single, *Terrifying*, was hurriedly commissioned instead. It didn't look particularly plant-like, but nobody minded – or even seemed to notice – because it looked good anyway. The colour scheme was adjusted as the tour went along.

Meanwhile, all the other specials on the Urban Jungle menu were cooking nicely. Despite the fact that both Steel Wheels and Urban Jungle boasted generous helpings of Stones' classics, neither show was merely a greatest hits package. The concerts were seriously roadtesting songs from *Steel Wheels*, the band's first album in three years. *Mixed Emotions, Sad Sad Sad,* and *Rock And A Hard Place* were in there most nights. *Blinded By Love, Almost Hear You Sigh* and *Terrifying* received regular airings. Keith usually sang *Can't Be Seen* alongside *Happy* in his vocal slot. Of the older tunes, Urban Jungle highlighted one notable absentee from the Steel Wheels set: the anthem for the inflatable doggies, *Street Fighting Man*, had been carefully dusted down and renovated to the same impeccably high standard as everything else.

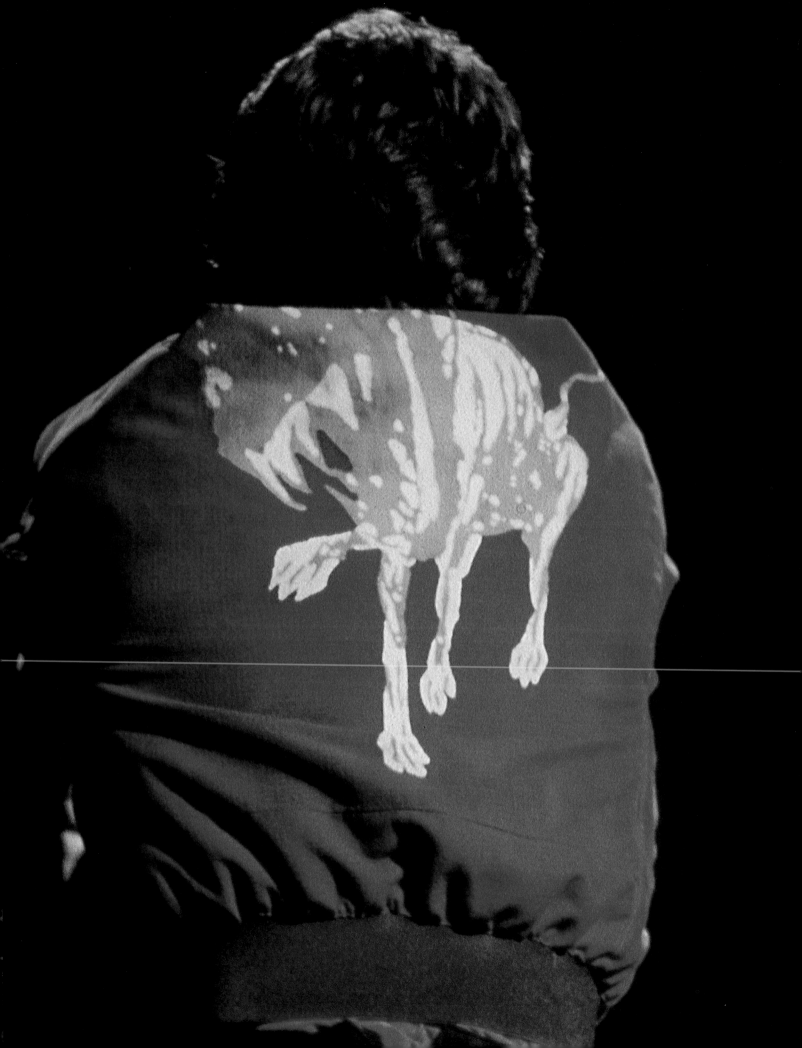

It was this fierce concentration on keeping the music sounding sharp and fresh which really saved the Urban Jungle show from turning into a modified, not to say scaled down, version of Steel Wheels. It would have been easy – and quite understandable – for the Stones to have done what nearly all stadium rock bands now do on The World Tour – drift onto automatic pilot, perform the same songs in the same order every night, line up plenty of backing tapes to airbrush away any sloppiness in the playing . . . and sleepwalk it.

They actually succumbed to none of those options. For the month of April before the European leg, the Stones were back in rehearsal at a chateau in Dangu, near Paris. There were the two new backing singers to drill, some new songs to straighten out and some old ones to reclaim. Whereas in the past the Stones might have left everything to intuition and that old live magic, for this tour they got down to work, painstakingly recreating all of the original arrangements rather than simply busking through an approximation of them. They would regularly

work all through the night to get a song absolutely right. Such was the case with *Street Fighting Man* which they played, straight through, no less than 18 times.

Jagger's view of the Stones' newfound commitment was characteristically sardonic. "There used to be tremendous ups and downs. We'd give a great show then a really substandard performance. People were being late for shows, not wanting to do sound checks. I think they thought being lackadaisical was kind of hip. But the tenor of the moment has changed. Now everybody seems really focussed and proud of what they're doing. It's more hip to be professional now."

Maybe it is. Certainly, the sheer professionalism of this show impressed some pretty unlikely people. One Major General Corbett of the Irish Guards paid a surprise visit to Patrick Woodroffe's lighting tower when the Urban Jungle tour played Berlin. The experience of witnessing Woodroffe passing instructions to his 35 pyro and lighting technicians left the good Major General in a bit of a daze.

Sound checks – Keith gives it a thrash, Ron gives it a scratch and Mick pauses for thought.

It was, he declared afterwards, so well organized it was "just like directing artillery fire."

The ultimate test of the Urban Jungle tour, though, was always going to be its popularity with European audiences. In the States, the Stones commanded unswerving loyalty. Closer to home, and with a recession on the way, nobody could be sure. It had been a long time, etc, etc. In the event, several European stadium shows by big international superstars actually had to be called off or re-scheduled inside smaller, indoor arenas during the summer of 1989; but not the Stones'. The "word of mouth" on this show was uniformly good. Dates were added in nearly every country to which it travelled.

In their own back yard, fickle Britain, the band played to more than twice the number of fans who had turned out in 1982 – a remarkable tribute to what can only be described as the survival of the fittest. Something to do with the law of the (urban) jungle, perhaps.

HONKY TONK WOMEN

The biggest stars of the show every night were, inevitably, the Honky Tonk Women, Angie and Ruby. 60 feet high when fully erect, they were made from four hundredweight of ripstop nylon and needed a tremendous amount of puff (180 cubic metres each, from two huge industrial air conditioning fans) to stay inflated. The problem, once they were up, was to stop them from floating away, as Pink Floyd's pig had done in 1976. A team of between 8 and 12 roadies – depending on the strength of the prevailing wind – was always in place behind the scenes, with guy lines, to make sure that the girls behaved themselves properly. And, despite snagging their stockings a few times on the way up and down, behave they did, to enormous applause. It's hard to see how the Stones will ever be able to perform this song again without them.

INFLATABLES

When the opening bars of *Honky Tonk Women* filled the stadium, Keith Payne's eyes were on the crowd. Those in the crowd, however, only had eyes for Ruby and Angie, the two 60 foot high hookers appearing as if by magic at each side of the stage. The girls were Keith's darlings and watching the audience react to them was always the high point of any show for him.

Ruby and Angie, as well as the rabid dogs which sprang up

stage was required. When it was time to say goodnight to the girls, the fans were thrown into reverse, sucking the air out to collapse the figures. They could then be packed into boxes little bigger than tea chests and the boxes (weighing four or five hundredweight depending on whether the ladies had got wet or not) were loaded onto the trucks for the journey to the next venue.

The dogs, Top Dog, Kennel Dog, Skippy and Shagger

to accompany the band on *Street Fighting Man*, were made by Air Artists of Suffolk, a company which has been creating inflatables for all kinds of stage shows for around 15 years. The inflatables were made from sections of ripstop nylon which were stitched together, then inflated and sprayed by Keith and the crew from his company, Air Brush, hanging from cherry picker crane platforms in the British Airship Industries hangar in Bedford.

On stage the biggest inflatables, the girls, took 30 seconds to inflate with an industrial air conditioning fan breathing life into them at a rate of six cubic metres per second. The air, of course, bled out through the stitching, so the fans continued to blast air into the figures for as long as their presence on

(Shagger contrived to eat Jagger during the show) were also Keith's responsibility. Despite the fact that there were guide cables to help ensure a trouble free inflation and the fact that an inflatable could have up to six roadies keeping it under control in a windy stadium, the dogs and the girls would occasionally foul the rigging and require running repairs and paint touch-ups.

Having taken less than a week to manufacture once the design process was completed, these simple, but highly effective stage props were, according to Keith, relatively easy to look after.

Once every show, Jagger just had to remember to feed Shagger.

To help the band relax on the Steel Wheels tour, pool tables were installed in the tented enclosures backstage. For Urban Jungle in the UK, these were replaced by more "British" snooker tables.

As well as pool or snooker tables, video games were available. To escape from the stress of being Mick Jagger, the Stones' front man would occasionally see how he coped with the pressure of being Nigel Mansel. How Nigel Mansel might feel about fronting the Stones is another matter.

MUSICIANS/BACKING SINGERS

There had never been so many "walk on" parts in a Stones' show as there were for this one. In the end, a carefully selected squad of 10 ancillary players, blowers and singers were needed to get the songs sounding the way the band wanted them – which was, in all cases, exactly the way they had been arranged and recorded in the first place. With no short cuts, and no backing tapes allowed, there was nearly always plenty of extra work to be done.

The most visible and attractive guests at the onstage party were the trio of black backing vocalists down at the front on the left. From Los Angeles to Poplar in East London via Queens, New York they came, trailing some interesting previous work experience. Bernard Fowler, from NYC, had taken time out from his day job with Tackhead, the uncompromisingly hard rock/dance outfit, to let his sweet tenor voice be heard more clearly on songs like *Ruby Tuesday*. Lorelei McBroom, from LA, was a singer/songwriter in her own right with a long list of "also sang" credits for artists such as Pink Floyd, Lou Reed and Billy Idol. Sophia Jones, from London, E14, had helped out U2 on their Rattle and Hum tour.

Sophia and Lorelei joined Bernard for the Urban Jungle tour, but for Steel Wheels he had enjoyed the company of two different young ladies. Lisa Fischer from Brooklyn had recorded with artists like Billy Ocean and Dione Warwick and toured with Chaka Khan and a certain Mr Michael Philip Jagger. Cindy Mizelle, from Englewood New Jersey, had - like Lisa - a host of impressive credits to her name. As well as writing and performing her own songs, she had accompanied Carly Simon, Melba Moore, Freddie Jackson and Chaka Khan to name but a few.

The horns looked rather more used and sounded a lot more familiar. The baritone sax man Bobby Keys had been playing regularly with the Stones for 20 years. Along with Jim Price, he had been their brass section, period, on most of the classic albums of the 70s. In 1988 he was signed up by Keith Richards for his solo project, the X-pensive Winos. For this tour Keys was joined by the four piece Uptown Horns, a curious looking quartet of no fixed haircut who could nevertheless deliver a fiercely brassy punch and who numbered James Brown and Tom Waits among their regular clients.

Over the course of the two and a half hour show, horn players and backing singers came and went, retiring to their respective cubby holes somewhere up inside the

Previous pages
(left) Sophia Jones, Bernard Fowler and
Lorelei McBroom lend the Stones some vocal
support.
(right) The Uptown Horns provide a blast of
brass and plenty of style.

(above) Matt Clifford gives Bill a better view.
(centre) Chuck Leavell
(right) Matt Clifford

vast Urban Jungle edifice when they weren't needed. The
Stones' two keyboard operatives, however, never left
their posts. Chuck Leavell, a veteran of the 1982 tour and
sometime Allman Brother, took care of the straight,
rhythmic piano parts: boogie woogying (*Honky Tonk
Women*) or rocking out (*Sympathy for the Devil*) as the
occasion demanded.

Young Matt Clifford, on the other hand, had a rather
different brief. Having been rescued by Mick Jagger from
the jaws of Anderson, Bruford, Wakeman and Howe – it

was his job to rummage through a bank of computerised keyboard and sampling equipment to find the orchestral voices needed for songs like *As Tears Go By*, *Ruby Tuesday* and *2000 Light Years From Home*. He also played the French horn at the beginning of *You Can't Always Get What You Want*.

The textural sophistication of the show relied heavily on the talents of the backing singers and musicians and the applause which was so warmly afforded them was richly deserved.

MIDNIGHT RAMBLER

Nothing in the whole performance demonstrated the band's confidence in their own musicianship better than this long and brilliantly paced account of the old rude blues favourite, *Midnight Rambler*. Jagger is usually judged on his dancing, his prancing, his dress sense and – sometimes – his singing. Here he served a belting reminder that he can still play the blues harmonica as well as anyone, and has now, thanks to his solo tour perhaps, become a pretty proficient rhythm guitarist into the bargain. The real beauty of this song lay in its quieter parts. In a sense, anybody can put together a big stadium show but few have the necessary charisma – or nerve – to leave the tricks aside and hold a vast crowd in thrall to just a voice and a guitar. There may have been more exciting moments in the show, but there were none more bold and magical.

To get from one venue to another on time, it was essential that the Stones had an aircraft on hand. In the States a Boeing 707 was at their disposal. For the band's various hops around Europe, aircraft charter brokers Chapman Freeborn laid on a selection of planes ranging from a 78 seat DC-9 to a 168 seat MD-3.

The Urban Jungle tour logo was the inspiration for the four rabid dogs which erupted onto the stage during *Street Fighting Man*. Everyone was determined that Urban Jungle should not give the impression of being simply a poor relation to Steel Wheels. The European show had to be a unique experience.

HAPPY

Everybody was playing better on this tour than they had perhaps ever played before, none more so than in the guitars department. Keith Richards' commitment to living rock and roll is surpassed only by his enormous enthusiasm for playing it. The frequent flash of that familiar grin was seen so often on the tour that there could be no doubt as to how much Keith was enjoying being back on stage with the Rolling Stones.

No one could have been more disappointed than Keith Richards, then, when two shows at London's Wembley Stadium had to be postponed when a septic finger put him out of action. Postponing the shows was an agonising decision, but an inevitable one. Offering a packed stadium in the Stones' "own back yard" a substandard performance was unthinkable, especially given how consistently well Richards had been playing.

Perhaps, like Jagger, Keith's stunning performances stemmed from the discipline imposed by his solo album and tour in 1988; maybe he was just on a roll. Either way, there was no mistaking the cocksure class of his playing this time. From the slashing opening of *Start Me Up* through to the steaming finale, *Satisfaction*, Keith was on the case, particularly so during the two song segment when Jagger left the stage to him. *Happy*, his vocal debut from *Exile On Main Street* was an obvious choice and crowd pleaser for Richards' solo spot.

Either *Before They Make Me Run (Some Girls)* or *Cant Be Seen* from *Steel Wheels*, provided the second number of the interlude before the Richards generator was back on line as the powerhouse behind the main performance.

FANS

It had been almost eight years since the band had last played live together and all the months of planning, preparation and rehearsal which went in before Steel Wheels took to the road proved that the Rolling Stones were determined not to disappoint their fans.

The fans, on the other hand, were just as determined not to disappoint the band. The capacity crowds in stadia on three continents included legions of stalwart Stones supporters from the sixties as well as younger fans, many of whom had barely been cutting their first teeth when the Stones were cutting their first record. Many, indeed, hadn't even been born in the sixties.

Bridging any real or imagined generation gap, the Stones

played to over six million devotees worldwide. Maybe some had dusted off a memory or two in recalling the lyrics of *Ruby Tuesday* or *Let's Spend The Night Together*, maybe some had the songs fresh in their minds, but none could have put more effort into singing along than the fans in Japan.

Learning songs verbatim from a recording sung in a peculiar dialect of a particularly difficult foreign language is a daunting undertaking, but the Tokyo Dome stood witness to thousands of fans chanting lines like:

I met a gin soaked bar room queen in Memphis
and
I was raised by a toothless bearded hag!

The Stones weren't performing alone at any show. They had the best support they could ever have hoped for . . . their own audience

Production Coordinator Michael Ahern (centre) talking to Mick Jagger and sound man Benji Lefevre.

SOUND

Steel Wheels and Urban Jungle were designed for maximum visual impact but the months of painstaking creative planning spent blending the stage concepts with the lighting design and the Stones' set list would have amounted to sheer folly if particular attention had not been paid to the sound system.

The man brought in to mastermind the audio arrangements was Benji Lefevre. With almost 25 years' experience of touring with rock bands, Benji had a shrewd idea of the sort of problems the band would face in taking such a massive stage show all around the world.

Lefevre looked to Showco, of Dallas, Texas, to supply the equipment he needed and with the two complete Steel Wheels sound systems on the road in the U.S., he needed plenty. Much of the hardware had to be specially manufactured for the tour.

Each show required 80 tons of sound gear transported in six 44 foot articulated trucks. A whole truck was required for the amps and sub bass speaker enclosures. Another carried the stage left speakers, another the stage right speakers and yet another took care of the stage monitors.

Lefevre's field delay system filled a truck all on its own. The digitally delayed speakers were mounted on carefully designed towers during a show, arranged with mathematical precision around the stadium to ensure an even and efficient spread of sound throughout the arena without obstructing the view of the stage for any of the audience.

The stacks on the stage itself reached up to a giddy 65 ft, again to ensure that those furthest from the stage could hear everything every bit as well as those right at the front. The stage was designed with a floored roadway below it specifically for moving the sound gear into position as quickly and smoothly as possible.

Two complete 10 man sound crews worked on the Steel Wheels stages in the U.S. as well as a universal team of six

who travelled from show to show. For Urban Jungle, a 12 strong team travelled from one venue to another. Each crew member spent two days at the rehearsal stage in Nassau learning exactly how the equipment should be installed and each was provided with a personal copy of the sound system design and wiring layout. Each of the crew had a specific job to do and it was imperative that they knew exactly where every element of the sound system should be for everything to be loaded in and out of the stadia efficiently.

To this end, the sound crews also had to work in harmony with the riggers and lighting crews. Cooperation was the key work in loading in and out of a stadium quickly. During the show Lefevre controlled the sound from his mixing desk, fine tuning the system at the same time to compensate for imponderables such as vagaries in the weather, whilst his crew monitored the equipment, poised, for example, to replace an amplifier on the spot should it begin to show problematic symptoms.

Wear and tear on the equipment was dealt with on the road. A technician travelled with the tour diagnosing faults and effecting repairs and maintenance on the electronics. Lefevre took a "hands on" role here, too, even turning his hand to a spot of carpentry when speaker cabinets, swollen by the rain, refused to fit into their alloted truck space. Essential spares were available to cater for maintenance which might put any element of the sound system out of action. Around 150 substitute speakers of different sizes were carried on the tour. Sending to Dallas for a replacement should something malfunction was out of the question.

Venues were also viewed with a critical eye when it came to maintaining sound quality. In Pittsburgh a 160 foot long glass fronted press enclosure was found to be reflecting sound to an unacceptable degree. The whole enclosure was simply masked off with specially made black drapes.

Throughout the whole tour the band, and especially Mick and Keith, were heavily involved with the sound crews, giving and taking advice and criticism with just one thought in mind; to stage the best possible Rolling Stones performance, and at the next gig, to make it even better.

2000 LIGHT YEARS FROM HOME

While nobody could accuse the Stones of being an art-rock band, the show did contain some bits which might have confused Chuck Berry, and *2000 Light Years From Home* was definitely one of them. Recorded in 1967 for the *Satanic Majesties* album, it had never been performed live before because of the problems involved in recreating that delicate swirl of sound which surrounds Jagger's psychedelic vocal. Now Matt Clifford's machines had sorted all that out, leaving the stage free for Mick Jagger to essay a spot of modern dance beneath one of Patrick Woodroffe's most strikingly atmospheric lighting designs. The choreography, like everything else, had not been left to chance or the inspiration of the moment. Jagger was coached for this languid, snakey routine by the British modern dance choreographer, Ben Craft and his American counterpart Lavelle Smith.

SYMPATHY FOR THE DEVIL

It's sometimes referred to as the "Cor! Fuck!" factor, and every Stones spectacular has to have one in it somewhere. It's the main *coup de theatre* of the evening, or, if you prefer, a colossally extravagant item of visual gimmickry. On the 1982 tour, it involved Jagger being plucked out of the PA stacks at the side of the stage by a cherry picker and whirled over the heads of the audience. For this outing, he was secretly whisked up to the top of the set in a special elevator to perform *Sympathy For The Devil* about a hundred feet or so above the rest of the band. A slightly risky stunt, which must have added considerably to the tour's insurance bill, it passed almost completely without mishap except at Hannover in Germany when Jagger's mike wouldn't work, forcing him back down again, sharpish.

IT'S ONLY ROCK AND ROLL

It may be a clichéd turn of phrase but this, maybe more than any other Stones hit certainly deserves its status as a "classic rock anthem". The timeless energy and raw edge of *It's Only Rock and Roll* belie the fact that the song is more than 16 years old.

Performing it on stage for this tour, the Stones had the best backing any rock band could imagine. To accompany the classic song, classic film footage filled the huge video screens at either side of the stage and the Stones cavorted alongside a host of rock heroes from Buddy Holly and Chuck Berry to David Bowie and Led Zeppelin.

Also up there on screen were the wan images of the '60s vintage Rolling Stones.

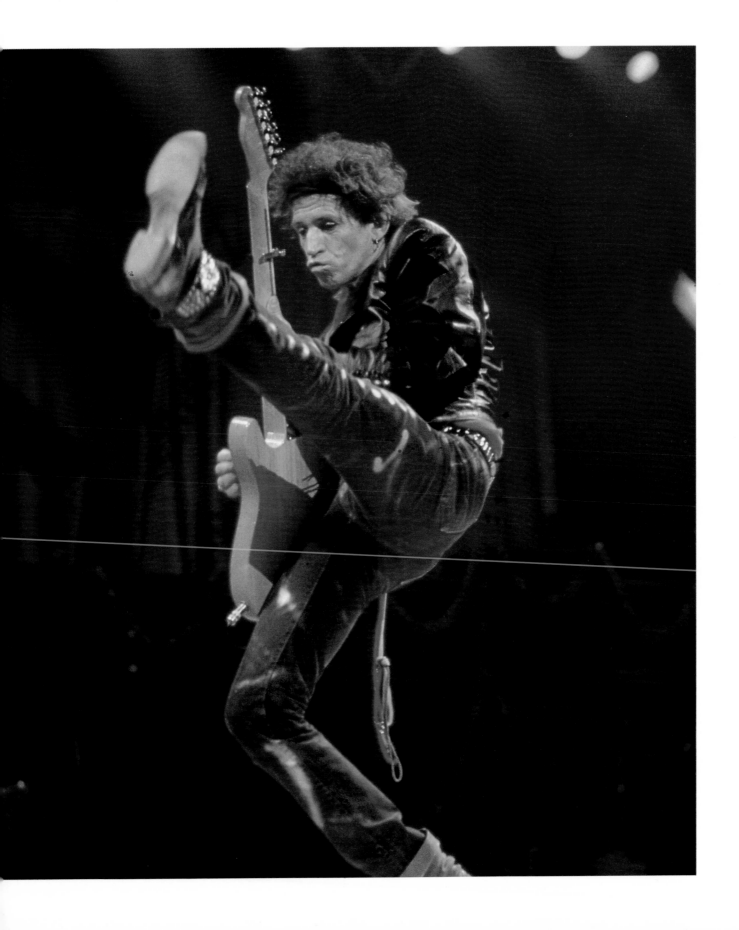

LOGISTICS

Moving Steel Wheels around America, Japan and Europe was like taking an army to war or, more accurately, like grafting an industrial complex onto a selected city then swiftly transplanting it to another.

Venues for the shows were vetted months in advance, not only for capacity, location or availability, but also to establish whether the city in question could actually cope with staging the show. Local labour requirements and the impact on the local infrastructure would be considerable.

Six days before the Urban Jungle show (ten for Steel Wheels) the advance guard would arrive to begin site preparation, putting up tents, installing offices, phone lines, catering and medical facilities and making sure that the locally hired machinery - fork lifts, scissor lifts, cranes, etc. - was in position.

The next day, 75 scaffolders would show up, just ahead of 11 truckloads of scaffolding (known as "steel"). Each truck could have two drivers, so already almost 100 newcomers would be looking for food, coffee, showers, soap, towels and a phone to call home. Work in the stadium during this period would start at around six in the morning and probably not end until around midnight.

Around noon on the day before the show, what became known as "the buses from hell" would arrive. Up to ten buses would disgorge around 150 tour personnel, most of whom had generally got out of the wrong side of the bed (or bus) and weren't in the best of moods. Although the coaches were well-appointed with beds, toilets, shower and cooking facilities as well as video systems, all the weary travellers really wanted to do *en route* was to get some sleep. When they spilled out of the buses they too were looking for food, coffee, showers, etc., etc.

Local labour in the form of stage hands and security staff could amount to 400, swelling the ever growing population of the Stones' emergent industrial sprawl still further.

By the time the rest of the stage set, the sound and the lighting trucks rolled in, parking space for up to 38 forty four foot articulated units would be taken up. The Scania, Volvo and Daf trucks would arrive at intervals of between half an hour and an hour, having left their previous venue in that order.

Everything was packed into the trucks in a specific order at one show and loaded out at the next destination in the same fashion. Many items were, in fact, dismantled and loaded as soon as their usefulness on stage was at an end as long as this didn't interfere in any way with the performance. The loading process was constantly updated. More hands were added here or a truck pack redefined there to shave vital minutes off the load in and load out times.

When the show was all over and the public were trooping home with *Satisfaction* still ringing in their ears, the mobile industrial complex was

already on the move. The circus which took six days to set up was loaded out in as many hours and "the buses from hell" were on their way to a new destination.

The logistical problems, of course, weren't all centred around just one location. At any one time the show could be touching four different cities with five different 30 ton sets of steel on the road. If the itinerary changed, eleven trucks headed for Italy might suddenly be required in Austria with all the requisite paperwork and official stamps in order for crossing a different border. If there happened to be a hold-up at a border post, a path could sometimes be smoothed through the

stony ground of bureaucracy with a few freebie t-shirts or albums. The truck team leaders had a ready supply specifically for that purpose.

The years of experience accumulated by the personnel involved were what made the whole operation hang together. The dedication and sheer enthusiasm of the tour staff were summed up by Steve Thomas, one of those with the unenviable task of solving problems before they occurred. When asked why he still loved the frantic nomadic lifestyle so much after more than 17 years on tour with rock bands, he replied, "Hell, it's better than selling shoes to fat women!"

GUESTS

The most important guests at any Rolling Stones show are the fans who fill the stadium but there are always plenty of personal friends and familiar faces (all big fans, too, of course!) whom the Stones will want to greet in person.

Pictured on these pages are just some of the celebrity guests privileged enough to have spent some time backstage with the band.

Top row (left to right) – Bruce Springsteen, Patti Sciaffa, Mick; Keith, Steve Winwood,

Bill; Keith, Eric Clapton; Tom Waits, Barbara Orbison.

Middle row (left to right) – W. Axl Rose, Charlie; Rob Lowe, James Belushi; Keith, David Bowie, Ronnie; Charlie, Ringo Starr.

Bottom row (left to right) – Mick with Michael Douglas, Anjelica Houston, Barbara Streisand, Meryl Streep, Jerry Hall; Charlie, Elton John, Mick; Michael Hutchence, Keith; Ringo Starr, Mick.

SATISFACTION

It was never supposed to end here. The final night of the Urban Jungle tour had been planned to come down somewhere in Eastern Europe; but Keith's infected finger put paid to that. The last two shows of the Stones' run at Wembley Stadium in July had had to be postponed because of the injury, and so it came to pass that the ultimate episodes in this 45 part European adventure unfolded back in England on August 24 and 25.

But the show that played Wembley for the second time wasn't Urban Jungle at all, it was Steel Wheels. As if they hadn't done enough already, the Stones were making a concert film to commemorate the whole expedition, and so had recalled the monstrous metallic fantasy which they'd last seen in Japan in January. Staging Steel Wheels at Wembley was, frankly, a headache. Local authority health and safety restrictions meant there could be no aerial fireworks at the end. And the pitch's natural turf wouldn't stand the greater weight of the set. And the concert had to be over by 10.30 pm. And so on. But it happened. Musically, little things went wrong, as they often can do when the Stones find cameras pointing at them, but the atmosphere on the Saturday night was as highly charged as at any rock concert in recent memory. Everybody knew that this thing which had taken up such an inordinate amount of cultural space for nearly a year was about to disappear for good. And, in a storm of golden fairy dust, it did.

TOUR PERSONNEL

(usa)

Ahern, Michael – Production Coordinator
Aleck, Patricia – Travel Advance
Allison, Mike – Sound Technician
Anderson, Rick – Lighting Technician
Armstrong, Tom – Site Coordinator
Bakal, Jerry – Carpenter
Baptista, Joe – Site Coordinator
Bark, Paul – Varilite Technician
Batty, Bob – Lighting Technician
Beck, Dennis – Staging
Bender, Bob – Security
Benjamin, Guy – Panni Projectionist
Berger, Bill – Carpenter
Bernett, Tim – Travel Advance
Boehning, Wayne – Lighting Technician
Bouman, John – Pyro Technician
Brade, Rowan – Security
Briggs, Randy – Panni Projectionist
Brown, John – Staging
Buess, Pete – Sound Technician
Callaghan, James – Security Chief
Campion, Edmund – Electrician
Campion, John – Master Electrician
Caraffa, Nick – Staging
Carroll, Bob – Rigger
Carter, Clay – Rigger
Carus-Wilson, Simon – Lighting Technician
Caston, Monica – Video Camera Operator
Chavarris, Patricia – Production Assistant
Chavarris, Paul – Production Manager
Clements, Caroline – Makeup
Cofield, Michael – Pyro Technician
Cohl, Michael – Tour Director
Collins, Benny – Site Coordinator
Combs, Gene – Staging
Compton, Collin – Varilite Technician
Condon, Jeff – Merchandising
Conyers, David – Sound Technician
Cooke, Steven – Inflatables
Damas, Stan – Police Liaison
Daniel, Peter – Video Projectionist
Debeauport, Pierre – Guitar Technician

Delahanty, Jim – Rigging Supervisor
Duncan, Gerry – Promoter Production Coordinator
Dunn, Alan – Logistics
Dunn, Arnold – Band Road Manager
Efron, Paul – Carpenter
Eike, Torje – Physiotherapist
Elder, Mike – Promoter Production Assistant
England, Mark – Lighting Technician
Epstein, Gary – Sound Technician
Farese, Michael – Carpenter
Farrugia, Sam – Carpenter
Fisher, Mark – Set Design and Art Direction
Fogel, Arthur – Assistant Tour Promoter
Fortune, Jay – Carpenter
Friedman, Neil – Assistant Tour Publicist
Garabedian, Michael – Carpenter
Garrett, Todd – Sound Technician
Gilleland, Jerry – Tour Production Manager
Gnesin, Fern – Dressing Rooms
Goldman, Donna – Production Office Coordinator
Graham, Kenny – Site Coordinator
Green, Colin – Lighting Technician
Grenier, Bob – Rigging Supervisor
Griffin, Neal – Video Projectionist
Guinness, Miranda – Assistant to Mr. Jagger
Harbin, Eddie – Sound Technician
Hatfield, Tim – Sound Technician
Haynes, Bruce – Electrician
Hendrick, Shane – Electrician
Hill, David – Varilite Director
Hooker, Rusty – Promoter Accountant
Horgan, William – Security
Howard, Jo – Assistant to Mr. Wood
Howard, Steve – Promoter Production Manager
Huffman, Dan – Sound Technician
Hurwitz, Bob – Tour Accountant
Jackson, Helena – Video Camera Operator
Jones, Dennis – Rigger
Jones, Nick – Merchandising
Kim, Uiyung – Pyro Technician
King, Elizabeth – Lighting Technician

King, Tony – Press Liaison
Kittrell, Beth – Administrative Assistant
Kleinberg, Bennett – Advance Tour Publicist
Kohorn, Mark – Carpenter
Lakota, Anne – Video Camera Operator
Lamb, Roy – Stage Manager
Lashells, David – Carpenter
Lazar, Shelley – Ticket/Credentials Coordinator
Lefevre, Benji – House Audio Engineer
Machado, Dan – Sound Technician
Magee, Church – Band Crew Chief
Magnason, Bruce – Staging
Mayne, Rich – Site Coordinator
McGinnis, Jeff – Sound Technician
McGuire, Dennis – Video Engineer
McLeod, Robin – Video Camera Operator
Moncrief, David – Sound Technician
Moncrief, Lon – Staging
Morphy, Dave – Lighting Technician
Newlin, Mark – Sound Technician
Nolan, Steve – Lighting Technician
O'Brien, Kevin – Varilite Technician
Ogilvie-Grant, Alex – Production Assistant
Olean, Steve – Rigger
Oliver, Bea – Carpenter
Panaci, Mic – Lighting Technician
Park, Jonathan – Set Designer
Parker, Steve – Inflatables
Patterson, Matt – Lighting Technician
Payne, Keith – Inflatables
Perry, Norman – Assistant Tour Director
Pickering, Robern – Wardrobe
Putnam, Jim – Sound Technician
Randel, Gary – Varilite Technician
Reaves, Ron – Sound Technician
Richardson, Shawn – Assistant Lighting Director
Richardson, Bob – Carpenter
Richie, Russel – Lighting Technician
Rickards, Joel – Lighting Techinician
Riggio, Jaye – Assistant to the

Rongo, Steve – Carpenter
Rosen, Mike – Carpenter
Russell, Tony – Assistant to Mr. Richards
Safari, Dimo – Photographer
Sakowicz, Joseph – Band/Entourage Luggage
Scovill, Scott – Video Projectionist
Seabrook, Joe – Security
Shepard, Dave – Lighting Technician
Shepherd, Stephen – Drum Technician
Sinclair, David – Electrician
Smith, Greg – Sound Technician
Smith, Lavelle – Choreographer
Stallbaumer, David – Production Manager
Stewart, Dan – Lighting Technician
Strand, Christine – Video Director
Sullivan, Brian – Merchandising
Sutherland, Angus – Guitar Technician
Swink, Ed – Staging
Tanzman, Linn – Press Representative
Thomas, Steve – Promoter Advance Coordinator
Thomson, John – Lead Carpenter
Thonus, Steve – Staging
Topeka, Andy – Keyboard Technician
Torffield, Marvin – On Air Projection
Towne, Andy – Video Projectionist
Townsend, Mary – Staging
Wade, Glen – Panni Projectionist
Wade-Evans, Chris – Monitor Audio Engineer
Ward, Scott – Pyro Technician
Ward, Scott – Rigger
Wein, Bob – Promoter Security Director
Wiesman, Michael – Lead Carpenter
Wetzell, Henry – Electrician
Whitt, Vinnie – Carpenter
Wille, Randy – Sound Technician
Williams, Fiona –Stylist
Wilson, Charlie – Lighting Technician
Woodroffe, Patrick – Lighting Designer and Art Director
Woolley, Timm – Financial Controller
Wright, Joe – Electrican

TOUR PERSONNEL
(europe)

Ahern, Michael – Production Coordinator
Allison, Michael – Audio Technician
Armstrong, Thomas – Site Coordinator
Armstrong, John – Staging Crew Chief
Ashurst, Peter – Staging Crew
Austin, Tracy – Catering
Bailey, Rob – Driver
Bakal, Gerald – Carpenter
Banks, Janet – Catering
Baptista, Joseph – Site Coordinator
Barad, Gerry – Merchandising
Barker, Henry – Driver
Barton, Nicholas – Varilite Technician
Batty, Robert – Lighting Technician
Bedigan, Pete – Driver
Bell, Peter – Pyro Technician
Bender, Bob – Security
Berger, William – Carpenter
Bernett, Timothy – Production Travel
Bollem, Micky – Driver
Brade, Rowan – Security
Brandner, Briggie – Hotel Advance
Bricusse, Paul – Driver
Brockman, Tim – Promoter Security
Bruford, Ian – Staging Crew
Bryce, Neal – Driver
Burke, Peter – Driver
Burns, Lil – Promoter Production Assistant
Calderon, Tracy – Camera Operator
Callaghan, James – Security Chief
Campion, Edmund – Electrician
Campion, John – Chief Electrician
Candles, Andy – Driver
Carter, Clay – Rigger
Caston, Monica – Camera Operator
Cheevers-Hunter, Mandy – Catering
Clarke, Steve – Driver
Claude, Aline – Administrative Assistant
Clements, Paul – Site Coordinator
Clements, Caroline – Makeup
Cody, Matt – Staging Crew
Cody, Tim – Staging Crew
Cohl, Michael – Tour Director
Collins, Les – Driver
Conafray, Mick – Driver
Conk, John – Site Coordinator
Conyers, David – Audio Crew Chief
Cooke, Jan – Driver
Cooke, Ystffan – Inflatables
Craddock, Terrence – Staging Crew
Craft, Ben – Choreographer
Crawford, Anne – Catering
Crust, Alison – Catering
Cubbin, John – Driver
Curtis, Lynn – Assistant to Norman Perry
Daniels, Peter – Video Projectionist
Debeauport, Pierre – Guitar Technician
Devenish, Val – Catering
Dickens, Terry – Staging Crew
Doherty, Bernard – Senior Press Representative
Drury, Gary – Driver

Dunn, Alan – Logistics
Dunn, Arnold – Band Road Manager
Edwards, Eddie – Starvision Technician
Efron, Paul – Advance Carpenter
Eike, Torje – Physiotherapist
Elstar, Elayne – Catering
England, Mark – Lighting Technician
Epstein, Gary – Audio Technician
Evans, Stretch – Staging Crew
Farrugia, Sam – Carpenter
Fellows, Mary – Production Assistant
Fennell, Mitch – Promoter Site Coordinator
Fennic, Bruce – Driver
Figley, Mary Lou – Promoter Site Coordinator
Fish, Suzanne – Catering
Fish, Marlene – Catering
Fisher, Mark – Set Design and Art Direction
Footit, Paul – Driver
Footman, Lorraine – Catering
Fortune, Jay – Carpenter
Fox, David – Driver
Franklin, Mike – Driver
Friedman, Neil – Press Representative
Gilleland, Jerry – Production Manager
Gnesin, Fern – Dressing Rooms
Goldman, Donna – Production Office Coordinator
Grabham, Sandi – Catering
Graham, Kenny – Site Coordinator
Graham, Mick – Driver
Gray, Alan – Pyro Technician
Green, Colin – Lighting Technician
Greenberg, Robbie – Varilite Technician
Grenier, Robert – Rigging Supervisor
Griffin, Neal – Video Projectionist
Guinness, Miranda – Assistant to Mr. Jagger
Hall, Stuart – Starvision Technician
Haltin, Paul – Driver
Hampson, Nicki – Catering
Harbin, Joseph – Audio Technician
Harkness, Desmond – Catering
Harrison, Tim – Driver
Hayward, Paul – Driver
Hill, David – Varilite Director
Hill, Dave – Driver
Hill, Mick – Driver
Hinde, Dave – Staging Crew
Hockabout, Eleanor – Promoter Production Assistant
Holcroft, Terry – Driver
Horgan, William – Security
Howard, Stephen – Promoter Production Manager
Howard, Jo – Assistant to Mr. Wood
Howell, Eric – Driver
Huffman, Daniel – Audio Techncian
Hunter, Ian – Catering
Hurd, John – Staging Crew
Hurlocker, Anthony – Electrician
James, Simon – Staging Crew
Jobson, Graham – Driver
Jones, Alan – Driver
Jones, Nick – Merchandising
Juggins, Graham – Driver

Keating, Tim – Staging Crew
Kennedy, Owen – Catering
Kent, Peter – Catering
Khan, Tariq – Staging Crew
King, Tony – Press Liaison
Kite, Ollie – Trucking Coordinator
Klvana, Cynthia – Production Assistant
Kohorn, Mark – Carpenter
Lakota, Anne – Camera Operator
Lawrence, Albert – Promoter Site Coordinator
Lazar, Shelley – Tickets/Credentials Coordinator
Leary, Steve – Staging Crew
Lefevre, Benji – Audio Engineer
Leonard, Emma – Catering
Lewis, Gary – Staging Crew
Lewis, Jon – Driver
Lowes, Linda – Catering
Luxford, Bud – Merchandising
Lythe, Gary – Staging Crew
Magee, Chuch – Band Crew Chief
Maggiore, Ian – Catering
Marsden, Roderick – Merchandising Accountant
Marshall, Baz – Driver
McIves, Ian – Driver
McManus, Robin – Staging Crew
Meereis, Paul – Driver
Moncrieffe, David – Audio Technician
Moole, Alan – Driver
Morgan, Tarquin – Staging Crew Chief
Moynihan, Chris – Driver
Mutton, Colin – Entourage Accountant
Nash, Julian – Driver
Neuegebauer, David – Camera Operator
Newlin, Mark – Audio Technician
Nolan, Daniel – Lighting Technician
Nolan, Stephen – Lighting Crew Chief
O'Brien, Terry – Driver
Ogilvie-Grant, Alex – Assistant Financial Controller
Oliver, Bea – Carpenter
Orsburn, Terry – Assistant to Mr. Wyman
Otremba, Bob – Video Projectionist
Park, Jonathan – Set Design
Parker, Steve – Carpenter
Payne, Keith – Inflatables
Peck, Simon – Staging Crew
Pelly, Danny – Driver
Perry, Norman – Assistant Tour Director
Pescod, Phillip – Staging Crew
Phillips, Timothy – Lighting Technician
Pirt, Chris – Driver
Putnam, Jim – Audio Technician
Radant, Christine – Production Travel Advance
Reis, Gregory – Camera Operator
Riggio, Jaye – Assistant to Michael Cohl
Robbins, Marc – Promoter Tour Accountant
Robinson, Thomas – Production Assistant
Robinson, Marcus – Varilite Technician

Roddy, Frank – Driver
Rongo, Stephen – Carpenter
Rufo, Celeste – Camera Operator
Rulter, Paul – Driver
Russell, Tony – Assistant to Mr. Richards
Richardson, Robert – Carpenter
Sakowicz, Joseph – Logistics Assistant
Saunders, Ollie – Staging Crew
Scovill, Scott – Video Projectionist
Seabrook, Joseph – Security
Sen, Jane – Press Representative
Shea, Paul – Driver
Sheldrake, Fleur – Catering
Shepard, Stephen – Drum Technician
Simcox, Brian – Driver
Simcox, Chris – Driver
Simpson, Phil – Driver
Simpson, Chris – Driver
Sloan, Alan – Advance Press Representative
Spieser, Tom – Staging Crew
Stallbaumer, David – Stage Manager
Stebulitis, Jed – Driver
Stengel, George – Staging Crew
Stokes, Suzi – Wardrobe
Strand, Christine – Video Director
Stuart, Daniel – Audio Technician
Sullivan, Jim – Merchandising
Sutherland, Angus – Guitar Technician
Sutton, Albert – Driver
Talbot, Denise – Catering
Taylor, Mick – Driver
Thomas, Treys – Promoter Production Accountant
Thomas, Stephen – Promoter Production Advance
Thomas, David – Catering
Thomas, Roger – Driver
Thompson, Chris – Driver
Thompson, Brian – Driver
Topeka, Andy – Keyboard Technician
Townsend, Andy – Staging Crew
Tupper, Carl – Driver
Underwood, Tony – Driver
Vernall, Steve – Driver
Wade-Evans, Christopher – Monitor Engineer
Walker, Greg – Staging Crew
Warnock, Neil – Booking Coordinator
Watts, Bill – Staging Crew
Watts, Ollie – Staging Crew Chief
Wein, Bob – Promoter Security Director
Wetzel, Henry – Electrician
White, David – Starvision Technician
White, Linda – Catering
White, Ray – Starvision Technician
Whitt, Vinnie – Advance Carpenter
Widowson, Derek – Driver
Wiesman, Michael – Assistant Stage Manager
Wille, Randall – Audio Technician
Williams, Fiona – Stylist
Wilson, Charlie – Lighting Board Operator
Wolters, Rande – Rigger
Woodroffe, Patrick – Lighting Designer & Art Direction
Woolley, Timm – Financial Controller
Wynne, Joseph – Staging Crew

TOUR PERSONNEL

(japan)

Ahern, Michael – Production Coordinator
Allison, Mike – Sound Technician
Armstrong, Tom – Site Coordinator
Bakal, Gerry – Carpenter
Baptista, Joe – Site Coordinator
Beck, Dennis – Steel Team
Bender, Bob – Security
Berger, Bill – Carpenter
Brade, Rowan – Security
Brandhorst, David – Steel Team
Brant, Doug – Lighting Technician
Brockman, Tim – Promoter Security
Calderon, Tracy – Camera Operator
Callaghan, James – Security Chief
Campion, Edmund – Electrician
Campion, John – Master Electrician
Carter, Clay – Rigger
Caston, Monica – Video Camera Operator
Clements, Caroline – Makeup
Cofield, Michael – Pyro Technician
Cohl, Michael – Tour Director
Conyers, David – Sound Crew Chief
Cooke, Ystffan – Inflatables
Curtis, Lynn – Assistant to Norman Perry
Daltz, Bob – Promoter Production Coordinator
Daniel, Peter – Video Projectionist
DeBeauport, Pierre – Guitar Technician
Delahanty, Jim – Rigging Supervisor
Dunn, Alan – Logistics
Dunn, Arnold – Band Road Manager
Efron, Paul – Carpenter
Eike, Torje – Physiotherapist
England, Mark – Lighting Technician
Epstein, Gary – Sound Technician
Faris, Bryan – Lighting Technician
Ferrugia, Sam – Carpenter
Fisher, Mark – Set Design and Art Direction

Fleming, Mark – Steel Team
Fortune, Jay – Carpenter
Gilleland, Jerry – Tour Production Manager
Gnesin, Fern – Dressing Rooms
Goldman, Donna – Production Office Coordinator
Green, Colin – Lighting Technician
Greenberg, Robbie – Varilite Technician
Grenier, Bob – Rigging Supervisor
Griffin, Neal – Video Projectionist
Guinness, Miranda – Assistant to Mr. Jagger
Harbin, Eddie – Sound Technician
Hill, David – Lighting Director
Horgan, William – Security
Howard, Jo – Assistant to Mr. Wood
Howard, Steve – Promoter Production Manager
Huffman, Dan – Sound Technician
Jackson, Helena – Video Camera Operator
Jones, Nick – Merchandising
Kerr, Mike – Steel Team
King, Elizabeth – Lighting Technician
King, Tony – Press Liaison
Klvana, Cindy – Production Assistant
Kohorn, Mark – Carpenter
Lakota, Anne – Video Camera Operator
Lazar, Shelley – Administrative Assistant
Ledwith, Patrick – Steel Team
Lefevre, Benji – House Audio Engineer
Magee, Church – Band Crew Chief
McLeod, Robin – Video Camera Operator
Miller, Michael – Steel Crew
Muncrief, Lon – Steel Team
Newlin, Mark – Sound Technician
Ogilvie-Grant, Alex – Assistant Financial Controller
Oliver, Bea – Carpenter
Park, Jonathan – Set Design
Parker, Steve – Inflatables
Payne, Keith – Inflatables
Perry, Norman – Assistant Tour Director
Randel, Gary – Varilite Technician
Rels, Greg – Camera Engineer

Richardson, Bob – Carpenter
Rickards, Joel – Lighting Technician
Riggio, Jaye – Assistant to Michael Cohl
Robinson, Tom – Steel Team
Rongo, Steve – Carpenter
Russell, Tony – Assistant to Mr. Richards
Scovill, Scott – Video Projectionist
Seabrook, Joe – Security
Shepherd, Stephen – Drum Technician
Skidmore, Paul – Steel Team
Smith, Lavelle – Choreographer
Stallbaumer, David – Stage Manager
Stingel, George – Steel Team
Strand, Christine – Video Director
Sullivan, Jim – Merchandising
Sutherland, Angus – Guitar Technician
Tanzman, Linn – Press Representative
Thomas, Steve – Promoter Site Coordinator
Topeka, Andy – Keyboard Technician
Torffield, Marvin – On Air Projection
Townsend, Mary – Steel Team
Wade, Glenn – Panni Projectionist
Wade-Evans, Chris – Monitor Audio Engineer
Ward, Scott – Pyro Technician
Ward, Scott – Rigger
Wein, Bob – Promoter Security Director
Wetzell, Henry – Electrician
Wiesman, Michael – Lead Carpenter
Wille, Randy – Sound Technician
Williams, Fiona – Stylist
Wilson, Charlie – Lighting Crew Chief
Wolters, Rande – Rigger
Woodroffe, Patrick – Lighting Designer and Art Direction
Woolley, Timm – Financial Controller
Wynne, Joseph – Steel Team

Special thanks to the following for all their help

Academy Costume, Valerie Adamson, Hiroshi Akiyama, Azzedine Alaia, Lawrence Anderson, Mace Bailey, Sterling Ball, David Bernstien, Peter Berry, Trish Biggar, Jay Black, John Branca, Mike Brown, Cliff Burnstein, August Busch IV, Chris Chapman, Marianne Colaneri, Brian Collings, Chris Combs, Joe Corcoran, Brian Croft, Janice Crotch, Dave Crump, Sherry Daly, Don Dawson, Dennis Davis, Malcolm Doak, Patricia Dupont, Gene Evans, Fred Feingold, Ken Fitch, Arthur Fogel, Annie Fowler, Bob Franceschelli, Gary Geller, Marion Goddard, Paddy Grafton Green, Lee Griffin, Adrian Gwillyin, Mike Hawksworth, Jane Hayes, Rob Harries, Richard Hartman, Lydia Hernandez, Steve Howard, Walter Howell, Penelope Hyer, Lynette Jackson-Lammers, Karen Kearne, Carol Kelleher, Sally Anne Kenneally, Paige Kevan, Chris Kelly, Kenji Kitatami, Michael Kovine, Cynthia Klvana, Howard Kushner, Rhona Levene, Richard Leher, William Ivey Long, Rupert Lowenstein, Mike Lynch, Robin Magruder, Matt Masciandaro, Barbara Maters, Bob McCann, Tony McCuaig, Bill McNulty, Peter Mensch, Hubert Michard–Pellissier, Michiko, Bill Miller, Sue Millership, Barry Mindell, Paul Minter, Isaac Mizrahi, Keith Morley, Aiden Mullen, Andrew Murray, David Nutter, Tim Norman, Sieji Osaka, Joe Owens, Sam Parker, Peter Parcher, Tony Perry, John Piersce, Sandy Powell, Mr and Mrs Charles Pozzo, John Richmond, Derek Michael Roll, Jane Rose, Nancy Rosenblatt, Dominique Sallembien, Mathilde Sandberg, Stuart Samuels, Noela Sanderson, Jim Schobell, Tim Schoem, Marlene Schwartz, Alan Selzer, Jay Sendyk, Hisatake Shibuya, Tommy Shigetomi, Edwin Shirley, Brent Silver, Linda Simmons, Howard Siuclare, Randal Smith, Claire Stone, Kevin Tooley, Seijiro Udo, Frank van Hoorn, Debbie Walker, Guy Wallace, Jerome Walton, Andrew Wilkinson, Steve Winter, John Wohlegemuth, Jamie Wood, Leah Wood, Tyrone Wood, Julie Fusella Woolley, Chris Wright, Yasmin at Jones, Lance Yates.